In Search of a Way

In Search of a Way

Two Journeys of Spiritual Discovery

GERARD W. HUGHES

Darton, Longman and Todd
London

Published in Great Britain in 1986 by
Darton, Longman and Todd Ltd
89 Lillie Road, London SW6 1UD

Reprinted 1986 and 1987

First published 1978 by E. J. Dwyer Publishers,
32–72 Alice Street, Newtown, NSW 2042, Australia.

ISBN 0 232 51694 4

British Library Cataloguing in Publication Data

Hughes, Gerard W.
  In search of a way: two journeys of
  spiritual discovery.——[2nd ed.]
  1. Spiritual life
  I. Title
  248.4′092′4   BV4501.2

  ISBN 0–232–51694–4

Phototypeset by Input Typesetting Ltd,
London SW19 8DR
Printed and bound in Great Britain by
Anchor Brendon Ltd, Tiptree, Essex

Contents

Preface to the Second Edition   vii

Preface to the First Edition   xi

1 A Question of Identity   1

2 Isle of the Sea   17

3 Cliffs of Fall   30

4 The Road to Paris   47

5 The Continent   61

6 Vézelay   85

7 Taizé: a Sign of Hope   93

8 Mountain Welcome   113

9 Light in the Darkness   130

10 Florence, Siena, La Storta   147

11 Down in the Engine room:
the Heart of the Matter   167

Maps

Weybridge to Rome   xii

Weybridge to Newhaven   46

Dieppe to Paris   60

Paris to Vézelay   72

Vézelay to Grenoble   94

Grenoble to La Spezia   116

La Spezia to Rome   146

Preface to the Second Edition

On the road to Rome in 1975 I had no intention of writing a book about my journey. On arrival in Rome I had a phone call from Anthony Dwyer, an Australian, who had come to Europe to set up a publishing business specializing in 'light theology', inviting me to write a book based on articles which I had written on the road for the English Catholic weekly, *The Tablet*.

When I began to write, I despaired. The new publishing company was unlikely to take off with my recurring theme, 'It was very hot. I was very thirsty. I walked 32 kilometres and my feet were sore.' But Anthony Dwyer was persistent, so I kept scribbling. Even when I started on topics other than hunger, thirst and blisters, I was still full of doubts. Voices from the past assured me that I had no sense of style, little feel for language, limited imagination and a slow mind. Loudest of all was the voice which said, 'How dare you set yourself to write on spirituality of which you know so little and fail to practise what you do know.'

One of my treasured possessions is a gift from a reader of *In Search of a Way*. He first wrote to me from one of HM prisons asking if, on his release, he might make a retreat at St Beuno's, a Jesuit Centre of Spirituality in North Wales, where I was working. He came, stayed for ten days and entertained us all with his accounts of life inside. A few months later he wrote again from another prison, enclosing a gift, an empty tobacco tin, encased in a beautifully crafted lining formed of matchsticks. There was a picture, modelled on the Shroud of Turin, pasted onto the inside of the lid. On the wooden lining on the outside of the lid there was a painting of the Papal logo commemorating the Pope's visit to Britain, Her Majesty Elizabeth II on one side of the logo and the Pope facing her on the other. There was a note saying that the sender had fashioned the box, but another reader of *In Search of a Way*, 'a wee forger friend from Glasgow', had done the painting.

I was delighted and encouraged by this gift, and by the variety of people – young and old, committed and uncommitted Christians of different denominations – who wrote saying that they had enjoyed reading the book and that they had found it helpful because it expressed ideas and reflections which they shared but had never put into words. It was this response which led me to another discovery which I am only beginning to explore.

The real obstacle on our journey to God is not heat, thirst, blisters, road blocks, or other people, but the inner workings of our own minds, our inherited and unquestioned ways of perceiving ourselves and the reality around us. These are the most threatening and frightening obstacles, and the most difficult to overcome. In the ten years since writing the book I have been able to observe this truth, for I have been giving the *Spiritual Exercises* to individuals who have trustingly shared with me their own inner lives and through them I have learned more about the inner journey.

This new discovery had come to me during the walk, but I had not understood its significance. At the end of each day's walking I used to make brief notes on the people I had met, the conversations, the ideas which had come to me. The people I met were mostly welcoming and kindly, but occasionally I would come to a village where the locals were abrupt and unhelpful. After a few weeks I came to realize that people were kind and welcoming when I was feeling full of life and my feet were not painful; when I was tired and my feet were hurting, then villagers were abrupt and unhelpful! At the time I had no idea that I was projecting my subjective state on to them and making condemnatory judgements, which seemed to me to be objective. It was only after I had written *In Search of a Way* that I began to see the connection between this habit of projection and my difficulty in trying to write

the book. Unconsciously I was selecting, from the past, disparaging remarks about my ability to write, which I had assimi-
lated into my own mind and way of perceiving, accepting
them as axioms to be obeyed and not questioned, and
projecting them on to my present task of writing. On the walk
I had caught myself projecting my thoughts and feelings on
to other people; later, when trying to write, I caught myself
projecting other peoples' comments from the distant past on
to me. I began to see that both habits of projection were
destructive distortions of truth, which can create imagined
enemies by projecting our ills onto others and blaming them,
while also leaving us feeling helpless and hopeless by
projecting on to ourselves the disparaging remarks of others.
This is not a new discovery: it has been known for centuries,
but it is when we begin to spot it operating in ourselves that
the discovery becomes exciting and all-important to us. I
hope that reading *In Search of a Way* may encourage readers
to embark on their own inner journey.

Is it not selfish to engage on an inner journey and to
encourage others to do so in a world where millions starve
through the greed of others and where our very existence as
a human race is threatened by nuclear weapons? It was
Einstein who said, 'The release of atomic power has changed
everything except our way of thinking and thus we are being
driven unarmed towards a catastrophe . . . The solution of
this problem lies in the heart of humankind.' It is our thinking
and our perceiving which must change. As individuals and
as a nation we tend to project our fears on to an enemy, in
our case the USSR, while the real danger, which is in our
own behaviour, continues to destroy us. In face of the threat
of nuclear annihilation we feel helpless, putting no trust in
ourselves and our own inner thoughts and feelings, where
God speaks, but entrusting ourselves to the experts who can
make us think we have nothing worth saying and that there
is nothing effective we can do. Projecting these assurances on
to ourselves, we become helpless and so 'we are driven
unarmed towards a catastrophe'.

Our journey is a journey of faith in God. Our sin lies in
not letting God be God, but choosing instead the false gods

who assure us that we are surrounded by enemies and are helpless and hopeless in face of them. May this book help the reader to recognize the false voices of the false gods, learn to ignore them, and listen instead to the voice within which is saying, 'Do not be afraid, for I have redeemed you. I have called you by your name and you are mine' (Isaiah 43:1), for 'his power working in us can do infinitely more than we can think or imagine' (Ephesians 3:20)

Darton, Longman and Todd gave me the opportunity to update *In Search of a Way* for this second edition. When I tried to do this I found I was writing another book, more rounded and tempered in style, but less true to the original experience, so I am content to leave it as written ten years ago, warts and all, apart from this preface and a number of editorial revisions kindly suggested by the publishers.

Birmingham 1986

Preface to the First Edition

This is a book about two journeys. One, on foot from Weybridge, near London, to Rome in the summer of 1975, lasted for ten weeks. The other journey is spiritual, and still continues. It was to find direction in this second journey that I undertook the first.

Before leaving Glasgow University, where I had been chaplain to Roman Catholics from 1967–1975, I was given a farewell party. It began with a Mass at 7.30 p. m. At 1.30 a. m. the following morning I was trying to steer the last guest to the front door, refusing his persistent offer of a crumpled sandwich from the pile he was holding in the crook of his arm. 'Where the hell are you going from here?' he asked. 'Walking to Rome,' I replied. He staggered, dropped some of the sandwiches and strained to focus on me. 'What the . . . hell do you want to do that for?' He was not what is termed in those parts 'a good practising Catholic'. 'I'll tell you later,' I said, showing him safely to the front door. Seconds after closing it with himself on the outside, I heard a click, then saw sandwiches dropping through the letter-box. I owe him an explanation, which is one reason for writing this book.

A few weeks after my arrival in Glasgow, a beautiful but alarmingly aggressive medical student called Laura had come to see me. 'Tell me about the Catholic God,' she asked. 'There is no such being as the Catholic God,' I began, 'there is only one God, the God of all men, and he is mystery.' 'What do you mean, "mystery"?' 'He is too great to be contained within our thought categories, within any human definition. He is always greater.' She looked puzzled. 'You sound a bit of an agnostic.' 'I think that every Christian must be a bit of an

xi

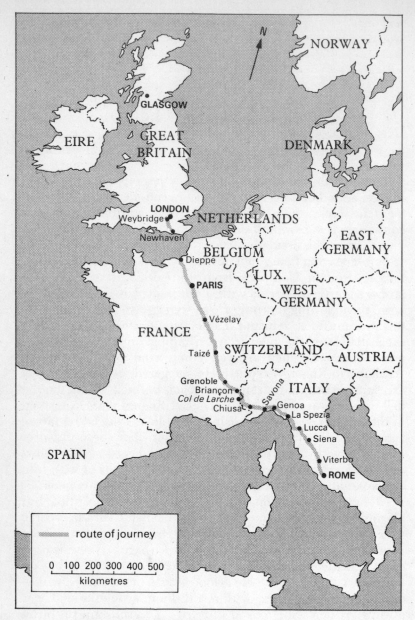

Weybridge to Rome

PREFACE TO THE FIRST EDITION

agnostic,' I replied. 'In scripture God says, "My ways are not your ways and my thoughts are not your thoughts." God is telling us through the prophet that we have to be a bit of an agnostic.' She no longer looked puzzled. She was ready to attack. 'Your Church', she said, 'does not give the impression of being at all agnostic. It seems to know infallibly through the Pope exactly who God is and how he acts, what and whom he likes and dislikes. He seems to like Catholics who go to Mass on Sundays, support the clergy, avoid contraception and obey the Pope. If you are as agnostic as you sound, you should not be a Catholic priest.' 'Nonsense,' I replied; 'if I do not acknowledge that God is mystery then I should not be a Catholic priest.' She had the last word: 'I don't think you really know who you are.'

I was not immediately disturbed by this remark. Like a depth-charge it exploded much later and it reverberates through this book.

I write out of my own experience, which was sometimes very painful. In writing of it, I run the risk of causing pain to others, whose experience and thinking is different from mine. I take the risk because out of the pain came hope, and that hope, which is for all of us, can unite us in our differences.

I dedicate this book to all my Glasgow relatives and friends. They equipped me for the journey. All that I wore and carried on my back was a gift from them. But they also gave me something which will remain when the boots and the camping equipment have fallen apart. For eight years they presented me with questions and challenges, problems and crises. They also gave me their friendship and laughter, the confidence to face the questions and the strength to survive the crises. They set me off in search of a way. This book is a small token of my gratitude.

I also thank Anthony Dwyer, who invited me to write this book, his wife Sue, who edited it so patiently, and the many friends who read the script and helped me with their suggestions and criticisms.

xiii

A Question of Identity

'The old man suddenly decided over a cup of coffee that he was going to call a Second Vatican Council. It will be a disaster, because he's totally disorganized.' This was the gloomy prediction of a German Jesuit, I was told, who had been an adviser to Pius XII, drafting some of his encyclical letters, and was now having difficulties with his faith in papal infallibility when Pope John XXIII no longer required his services! But the Holy Spirit can work through a disorganized man drinking a cup of coffee as well as through an organized man on his knees, and the Second Vatican Council was called.

In a book written in 1963, after the first session of the Council, Robert Kaiser began his account with the story of a Florentine painter who came to Pope Adrian VI in 1523 with his masterpiece entitled 'The Barque of Peter'. The painting showed the barque lifted above the waves by angels blowing eschatological trumpets. The waters beneath the ship were calm but, all around, the waters were whipped up in fury, full of drowning heretics, schismatics and sinners. The Pope sat on the top deck, his arms folded and eyes closed in a spirit of profound recollection, surrounded by his curia, household and guards. The faithful peeped out from their little square portholes down below. The sails were limp, but the papal flag stood out on the mast. The rudder was raised out of the sea and around it three figures read a Bible, opened at the illuminated text: 'Thou art Peter, and upon this rock I shall build my Church.' Pope Adrian is said to have been horrified. 'This is not my ship. Put it on the seas, fill the sails, dip the rudder into the sea and let me steer the bishops and their flocks and be saved with these drowning heretics, schismatics and sinners.' Soon afterwards Pope Adrian, a Dutchman and the last non-Italian pope, died. Some said he had been poisoned.

Robert Kaiser's thesis is that the Catholic Church remained very much as the Florentine painter had depicted it – above the waves, safe, secure and well organized, until Pope John XXIII arrived with little more than an oar on his shoulder and a spark of intuition in his heart and decided it was time to launch the boat and sail the high seas again.

To continue Kaiser's metaphor! The launching took place at the Second Vatican Council and the clerical crew have been feeling seasick ever since. Now the ancient barque is pitching and rolling on the uncharted seas of the twentieth century, where tides and currents change rapidly and unpredictably. The ship is not only creaking and leaking, she seems to be disintegrating. Her timbers are yawning, her crew growing mutinous and she no longer responds to the rudder. The people of God, formerly content to sit below deck enjoying their good fortune as they contemplated the fate of sinners, heretics and schismatics abandoned to the waves while they were safely steered to their heavenly port, are now growing restless and demanding a say in the running of the ship. But their language and theories of navigation are foreign to those of the clerical crew and the ship is so constructed that there are no easy lines of communication between the lower and the upper deck. There is also conflict within the same deck. There are those on both decks who feel that shipwreck can only be avoided by a sharp tack to port (the New Left in the Church), while others are equally convinced that unless the ship moves well to starboard, she will be wrecked on the rocks of Communism and Humanism. There are also those who think that in an emergency the only tactic is to batten down the hatches, heave to and wait for the storm to pass. In this crisis some, preferring the company of the heretics and schismatics, have chosen to jump overboard, while others, remaining on board, believe that the only hope of survival is to push overboard any who tend to rock the boat.

In 1967, two years after the Second Vatican Council had

2

ended, when the barque was beginning to pitch and toss, I was appointed Catholic chaplain in the University of Glasgow.

The West of Scotland area, of which Glasgow is the centre, has a Roman Catholic population of about 800,000, the largest concentration of Catholics in Britain and largely of Irish origin. The Irish came over to Scotland in vast numbers in the mid-nineteenth century, poor, uneducated, hungry – my own grandfather among them. They lived in slums, an alien Catholic people in a proudly Protestant country. They worked at the most menial tasks, suffered religious discrimination and were considered very second-class citizens. Shortly after my arrival in Glasgow I attended a function where I was introduced as a Catholic priest to a very Presbyterian lady. She tried her best, 'The woman who does my cleaning is a Catholic and a more honest, hard-working woman it would be hard to find.'

For the Irish immigrants to Scotland the Catholic faith was their identity, and the priests, usually the best educated among them, were their champions. 'Irish' became synonymous with 'Catholic' in the West of Scotland and 'Catholic' with 'Irish', to the detriment of both. At first, the immigrant children were educated in Protestant schools, but soon the religious orders, including the Jesuits, began to open schools for Catholic children.

In 1918, by an Act of Parliament, Catholics were granted their own schools, completely financed by the local authority. Today, Catholics form 40 per cent of the population and 50 per cent of the children of primary school age. The majority of the Catholic population is still working class. In Glasgow University, for example, less than 10 per cent of the teaching staff were Catholics in 1975. But the Catholic undergraduate body increased rapidly every year and formed 25 per cent of the students in 1975, numbering over 2,000, as compared with a few hundred in the 1950s. There is, consequently, a growing Catholic middle class.

Catholics in the West of Scotland during the nineteenth century looked on themselves as a beleaguered minority. They were naturally defensive, protective of their own and

3

suspicious of those who were not. Catholics there today are no longer a beleaguered minority, but like any other local Church throughout the world it is subject, like its Lord, to temptation, and the more powerful the Church becomes, the more it is in danger.

Christ was tempted. The Church too must expect to be tempted. Christ's temptations were subtle and came under the appearance of good. The Church's most serious temptations also come under the appearance of good. Christ was sinless. The Church is not. Therefore she must continually do penance, that is, turn back to Christ and his teaching, judging and reforming herself in the light of the gospel, her norm and her authority, to which all her members from the Pope downwards are subject. The Second Vatican Council was, in this sense, an act of penance of the Catholic Church. She needs this penance because she is always in danger of idolatry, of forgetting her meaning, which is to be the sign of God's love for men, becoming absorbed instead in her own survival as an organization, when maintenance becomes more important than mission.

Christ's temptations in the desert are the temptations to which the Church and all men will always be subject.

Christ was hungry after his fast in the desert. The tempter made the very reasonable suggestion, 'If you are the Son of God, turn these stones into bread.' It was a temptation to use his power, his status, to his own advantage. Perhaps it also included the temptation to win followers by providing them with free bread, as the Roman emperors used to do. It was the temptation 'to have for yourself', 'to possess for yourself', and Christ answers: 'Man does not live by bread alone, but by every word that comes from the mouth of God.' It is a subtle temptation because to have, to possess, is not wrong. But having, possessing, easily develops into greed, when possessing becomes the predominant value in life to which every other person and thing, even God himself, is made subject. This temptation was the downfall of medieval monasticism. It is still a temptation in the Church. When the Church begins to succumb, the content of its preaching is aimed at fund-raising and an increasing number of its clergy become preoccupied with the upkeep, administration and increase of Church property. The temptation is not limited to financial wealth or real estate. It is the temptation to build a security around ourselves which is not God. A sign that the temptation is succeeding is growing fear in the Church, fear of criticism, fear of freedom, fear of truth; she becomes a Church of warnings rather than a Church which proclaims the Good News.

Christ was tempted to leap off the pinnacle of the temple, which seems a very curious temptation at first sight. 'If you are the Son of God, throw yourself down, for Scripture says, "He will put you in his angels' charge." ' It is a reasonable temptation. Why not put on a show for people, if you really want to convince them? Dazzle them with wonders and miracles. The Roman emperors knew the wisdom of this advice and so they gave their people circuses as well as bread. Christ answers, 'Thou shalt not tempt the Lord thy God.' He refused to coerce men and women, to dazzle them with wonders. He wanted to win them by his love, not blind them by wonder-working. He wanted to empower them, not have power over them, to set them free, not to enslave them. This second temptation is the temptation to power over men, and Christ rejects it. The Church will always be tempted to power over men. Professional religious men are especially subject to this temptation because in virtue of their profession they can control the very core of the human person, the soul. The Roman emperors knew the enormous political advantage to be gained by declaring themselves to be divine. When the Church succumbs to this temptation, she preaches fear of damnation more than hope of salvation, exhorts to obedience and loyalty rather than to charity and truth.

In the third temptation the devil showed Christ all the kingdoms of the world and their splendour. 'I will give you all these', he said, 'if you fall at my feet and worship me.' This was the final temptation, the temptation 'to be', independently of God; the temptation of pride. Jesus replied, 'Be off, Satan! For the Scripture says, "You must worship the Lord your God, and serve him alone." ' Men and women are not absolute, thank God. They are something much greater,

5

called beyond themselves to transcend themselves. To deny God is to deny people. Human beings must worship and they become what they worship. People are made for God, and to worship any creature is to bring about their own destruction. This final temptation of Christ is the temptation to idolatry. Idols may be wealth, or power, or something much more subtle. Within the Church herself there is always the temptation to forget that she is a sign of God's love and to make herself an absolute. As this happens, she will become a closed Church, a Church which does not listen nor try to read the signs of the times. Being self-sufficient, she feels no need to listen, to learn, to change. She grows blind, bigoted and arrogant.

Every man, every Christian, every local church is subject to these temptations and the church in Glasgow was no exception. Because it was the church of a people who had had to struggle to preserve their identity, it tended to emphasize denominational differences (as though they were more important than the truths which all Christians share in common), and to hold tenaciously to its own specifically Catholic institutions. Any criticism or questioning of the value of specifically Catholic schools, for instance, was considered a mark of weak faith and of disloyalty.

It was not surprising that the Second Vatican Council, with its emphasis on the openness of the Church and its Decree on Ecumenism, should have met with a mixed reception in the West of Scotland. 'Don't worry, nothing has changed,' was the reassuring comment of one Scottish bishop to his people at the end of the Council. But many priests knew otherwise. 'We've gone Protestant,' they said. There is a story that after the Council, when Celtic, the Catholic football team, met their Protestant rivals, Rangers, a Celtic supporter encouraged his team with a new cry, 'Get tore intae yir separated brethren, Celtic!' Ecumenism had arrived in Glasgow and this was the manner of its coming.

My appointment as chaplain to Catholics in the University of Glasgow was made by the Archbishop of Glasgow in consultation with the Jesuit provincial. I had spent the previous seven years teaching at Stonyhurst College, a Jesuit public school, which in English terminology means a private, fee-paying school. Although I enjoyed the Stonyhurst years, I was glad to return to my native Scotland, which I had left for schooling in England thirty years before. But I had another reason for welcoming my appointment. Before beginning theology in 1955, I had already become interested in ecumenism. After one year's theology in England, I was allowed to do the remaining three years in Frankfurt, to study Protestantism at source. After ordination to the priesthood in Frankfurt and before my final years of theology, I asked my German superior if I might visit Scotland. 'Why?' he asked. 'Because it is my home,' I replied. He looked puzzled. 'You must have an academic reason,' he said. 'I'm very interested in Scottish theology,' was my answer and permission was readily granted.

After theology I wanted to do further study in ecumenism and then work in Scotland, but I was sent to Stonyhurst instead. I had kept up my interest in theology and arrived in Glasgow full of hope and my head filled with ideas culled from the Council documents, Karl Rahner, Yves Congar and Teilhard de Chardin. On arrival, I was delighted to see that the Catholic chaplaincy, called Turnbull Hall after Bishop Turnbull, founder of the University in 1453, occupied one end of a terrace, the opposite end being occupied by the Orange Lodge with the University Divinity faculty lying in between. It looked a promising omen.

The chaplaincy was a large four-storey building, which included a basement flat for a caretaker, a ground floor with a chapel which could seat 200 comfortably and often took nearly twice that number, offices, library, a student lounge and meeting rooms. The first floor had a large hall and a canteen, which served lunches daily in term time. The top floor contained rooms for chaplains and a few rooms for resident students.

Although the chaplaincy facilities were excellent, the Catholic students, mostly from the West of Scotland, showed a marked reluctance to use them. Provided Mass was said there on the few holy days of obligation in the year, which they attended in vast numbers, many of them could not see any

7

purpose in having a chaplaincy. Their religious teaching in Catholic schools, by providing answers to questions which they had not yet asked, had stifled the spirit of religious inquiry in many of them. There were some regular student visitors who appreciated a quiet and peaceful meeting place. And the library table, if suitably stacked with nineteenth-century religious books down the centre, could make a useful table tennis surface with a variety of games to be played with periodicals or hardbacks for bats.

Glasgow students are different in many ways from their English counterparts. In Glasgow, most of the students live at home and not on the campus. The men students tend to be reticent, almost as though they are ashamed of owning any knowledge not concerned with drink and football. The girls are also more shy than their English counterparts and take examinations, which in Glasgow are plentiful, very seriously. These first impressions can be very misleading if reticence is interpreted as lifelessness and football and drink talk as philistinism. The students I met in 1967 and later were lively and intelligent, friendly and responsive. Although most of the Catholic students I encountered were very critical of Catholicism as they had met it in their schools and parishes, their Christian faith was very important to them and they wanted to understand it. With Father Dominic Doherty, who worked with me for two years, we put on conferences, lectures, discussion and study groups, retreats and all-night vigils, and there was plenty of social life as well. Numbers grew and a community began to form, which included Catholics and Protestants, students and non-students, foreigners and Scots. One Sunday night after Mass, when there had not been enough room for everyone in the chapel, a Protestant student said to me: 'You will have to do something about the numbers.' 'What do you suggest?' I asked him. 'Tell the Catholics not to come and leave it for us,' was his reply.

Besides activity within the chaplaincy and university, I used to try to keep Saturdays free for hill-walking. I would put a notice on the board during the week, suggesting the hill and starting time, leaving space for the names of any who wanted to come, hoping we could find enough cars. In less than an hour by car from Glasgow there are magnificent ranges of hills and mountains. Hill-walking is an acquired taste, but once acquired it becomes an addiction. 'Great things are done when men and mountains meet,' wrote Blake, and the greatest thing that happened were the friendships formed on mountain climbs.

After one climb in 1970 we were recovering over a cup of coffee in the lounge at Turnbull Hall when a young couple came into the room and asked if they could see me privately. I was tired and in no mood for problems. I presumed they were students wanting to get married in spite of parental opposition to a mixed marriage. 'I'm Harry Campbell,' said the man, 'and this is my wife, Cathy. I hear you are looking for an occupant for the caretaker's flat and we are interested. I have to spend hours travelling to the university every day and I'm looking for something closer.' 'It is a tiny flat and very gloomy in the basement,' I warned them. By this time we were moving towards the front door where three small children were standing. I was introduced to the Campbell family, Heather aged 7, Stewart aged 6 and Lesley aged 4. They looked far too good to be true. They were all three fair-haired, blue-eyed and smiling. When I began teaching, one old priest had told me, 'the fairer the hair and the bluer the eyes, the more of the devil is in them'. 'You will never fit into that tiny flat downstairs,' I told them. 'We are willing to try,' said Harry. They came a few months later and stayed for five years. Whenever I read books or attend conferences on religious renewal, the importance of community etc., I think of the Campbells. They did not have time for conferences or to read big books. They kept open house in their tiny basement flat, students streamed in and there was always laughter, food and a cup of tea. I preached the Gospel upstairs and they practised it downstairs. The children became part of the place, were never a nuisance and were perfectly at ease in adult company.

When the school doctor recommended some treatment for Lesley, then aged six, she was able to inform him that a medical friend of hers had recommended the opposite. Stewart, a most precocious child, could beat most students

9

at chess, infuriating them because he sucked a lollipop during moves and read a book between them. The only person who could infuriate Stewart was his sister Lesley and he complained one day to his mother that he found Lesley a 'socialist embarrassment'. Heather was the peacemaker. When life became hectic and I grew over-serious, the children, intent on their latest game, would remind me of my distorted priorities. 'Unless you become as little children . . .' They trusted that the facts were kind and knew they were protected. Cathy ran the chaplaincy canteen and then became secretary. She had time for everyone and believed time was for people, not people for time, a wisdom I found difficult to learn. She thought nothing of staying up all night on one occasion to nurse one of the children's pet mice, which eventually passed away as dawn was breaking.

Harry and Cathy unwittingly taught me more pastoral theology by their lives than I had learned from books. They lived for their children, not out of a sense of duty, but because they seemed to find doing so the most natural thing in the world. They delighted in them, in their growing and learning; they played with them, suffered with them, laughed with them and considered them the most important people in the world. 'If you, then, who are evil, know how to give your children what is good, how much more will your Father in heaven give good things to those who ask him.' The Campbells helped me to pray the Our Father. The children addressed me as 'Father Shoos'. The title 'Father' with which priests are addressed can easily become as formal and impersonal as 'Sir'. Living with this family I began to see how much I had to learn from them about my role as a priest, as 'Father'.

'I don't think you know who you are.' Laura's remark made in 1967 lay dormant in my memory until it exploded a year later, in October 1968, a few months after Pope Paul had issued his encyclical *Humanae Vitae*, which reiterated the Catholic teaching that artificial contraception is 'intrinsically wrong'. 'Intrinsically', we had been taught, means that under all possible, imaginable circumstances contraception is wrong. According to the traditional moral books, there are

10

reasons which could justify the taking of human life in self-defence, or in a just war, or as a punishment for a grave crime, but nothing could justify contraception. I could not see the validity of the arguments given against contraception in the encyclical, but it was not philosophical arguments which worried me. I was worried at the effect the teaching was having on the lives of people who came to discuss the question. As they talked openly, I began to see with horror the suffering, and sometimes the tragedy to human life caused by this phrase 'intrinsically wrong'. I was meeting good, generous and sincere married people whose marriages were breaking up over this question and whose love for each other and for the Church was turning to hate.

I knew that the encyclical had not been presented as an infallible teaching and that it was, therefore, fallible, but I thought that I should let the Archbishop of Glasgow know of my difficulties because I was teaching moral theology, part-time, at a Catholic College of Further Education and I was also giving a course in medical ethics to medical students. I explained my position in a letter, and a week later the Archbishop invited me to visit him. We discussed the question for about an hour. A week later I was informed through an intermediary that the Archbishop wanted me to leave the chaplaincy at the end of the Christmas term 1968, and that meanwhile I must be silent both about my dismissal and the contraception problem.

At first I was benumbed by the news, but numbness gave way to a mixture of feelings: pain, confusion, frustration and anger. How was I to act? In obedience to my conscience or to the papal encyclical? I had no problem in answering this question. The problem and the pain lay in a further question: 'How do I know that my conscience is trustworthy, that I am not muddled in my thinking and blind through my own sinfulness?' I had theoretical answers to all these questions, but they did not dispel the self-doubt.

I went to London to see the Jesuit provincial. He negotiated with the Archbishop and on the last day of term, seven weeks after my dismissal, I was told that the Archbishop would

11

allow me to stay on and he never mentioned the subject to me again.

A university chaplain's job is very unstructured, ill-defined, and suited me well because I could meet a large number and variety of people of all denominations and none. Much of my time was spent in chatting to individual students and staff, and I became increasingly aware of the gulf that lies between the clerical and the lay world, between the theologian and the man in the pew. In these interviews I saw into a world in which Christian faith, far from being the Good News, was a message which made many people fearful of life. Many of those with whom I talked had abandoned the practice of their faith or were about to do so. They were not rejecting God, but a deformed image of God, a God of wrath and vengeance, interested only in their failures and sins. Until this false image of God is exorcized, faith cannot grow.

At first, although I enjoyed discussion with groups and individuals, I used to feel nervous in case I gave wrong advice, or weak arguments, or failed to convince them on some point or other. Later I came to realize the futility of trying to communicate the Church's teaching until I had listened carefully to their own opinions. They grumbled and criticized, then criticized their own criticisms, became more confident, more ready to listen and to question for themselves. They began to work more with other Christian denominations and to engage speakers of all denominations and none for lectures and discussions. One of their favourite speakers was Jimmy Reid, then a communist shop steward in the Upper Clyde shipyards, who was later elected rector of the University by student vote. Jimmy was at his most eloquent when commenting on the Sermon on the Mount. Another favourite speaker was Professor Barclay, the well known Church of Scotland scripture scholar.

Many of the people who came to see me were engaged couples of different denominations. The Catholic Church has a ruling that in the case of a mixed marriage the non-Catholic partner should have some instruction on the nature of Catholicism. It is a sensible ruling, which can help the couple towards a better mutual understanding, and I always advised the Catholic partner, if engaged to a practising non-Catholic, to have similar instruction from a non-Catholic minister.

To those not acquainted with Northern Ireland or the West of Scotland, the problem of mixed marriages can be hard to understand. I met Catholic and Protestant girls and boys who had been thrown out of their homes because they were going steady with someone of a different denomination. I met one Catholic teacher who was advised to resign from her Catholic school because she was engaged to a Protestant. The root of the problem goes back centuries and the divisions are kept alive in Glasgow by the separate schools, separate youth clubs and by a religious teaching so presented that by emphasis on the differences, the central truths of Christianity, which we hold in common, are neglected. When couples do get engaged across the denominations, there are usually grave warnings from parents and clergy on either side. When the couple marry and have a quarrel, the danger is that they interpret their differences as being religious, a misfortune beyond their control, and the marriage breaks up. Parents and clergy then shake their heads and say, 'We told you so', without reflecting that they may possibly have helped to make it so. God does not seem to be half so concerned about mixed marriages as are many of his ministers, because Catholics and Protestants keep falling in love. If two people who are in love cannot form a church of the home across the denominations, then there is little hope for the unity of the Church.

As chaplain I was not allowed to deal with the official marriage papers, nor to celebrate weddings in the chaplaincy. The couple had to go to the parish priest of the Catholic partner. Many of the parish priests were excellent and showed understanding, but others did not.

I came into conflict with some of the local clergy over marriage cases, was held to be the agitator behind the scenes of catholic student activities, to be modernist and humanist in my views and, cruellest cut of all, 'a so-called intellectual'. 'Satan's smoke curls through cracks in Peter's barque' were the heavy headlines in a Scottish Catholic newspaper. The writer condemned various priests in a paragraph, one because he had attended a hippie meeting at which 'pot' was smoked, another because he had taken part in an anti-Vietnam war demonstration, and I was given two paragraphs for my failure to protest publicly in the name of the Church at student lapel badges, issued for Charities' Day, which the writer considered to be obscene.

At first I was unaware of the criticism and rumours of my unorthodoxy, but after an anonymous and very abusive phone call, the substance of which was 'we are going to drive you out of Glasgow', I mentioned these rumours to the Archbishop, who had always treated me kindly since the 1968 episode. He told me to ignore them and reminded me that Glasgow was always full of rumour.

In 1972 I wrote a paper for a meeting of Catholic chaplains to Scottish universities. In the paper I described my own practice at Masses to which other Christian denominations had been specifically invited, namely, that I always explained the Catholic ruling on intercommunion before the Mass began, but if any non-RC then came to Holy Communion, I would not refuse, on the grounds that the damage done to unity by refusing would far outweigh any possible advantage in keeping to the ruling. The Archbishop read the paper, disapproved of my practice and forbade me ever, under any circumstances, to give Holy Communion to anyone who was not a Catholic. A few weeks later the Archbishop told the Jesuit provincial that I must be withdrawn from the chaplaincy. No reasons were given either to the provincial or myself.

I took advice from friends, tried but failed to have an interview with the Archbishop, and eventually informed the congregations at Masses on Whit Sunday that I had been dismissed. The dismissal hit the press, both local and national. There was a flurry of activity and interviews between the University and the Archbishop. At the end of a week of negotiations I was reinstated for a year, after which my position would be reviewed. I stayed on for another three years.

This dismissal was at once the most disturbing, but also the most encouraging experience I had known as a priest. It was disturbing because it raised that painful comment, 'I

14

don't think you know who you are' in more acute form than before. Many of the clergy thoroughly disapproved of what I had done. According to them I should have accepted the dismissal quietly and gone off to other work without a word to anyone. Making the matter public seemed to them disloyalty to the Church. I, too, believe in loyalty to the Church: that is precisely why I let people who formed the Church know exactly what was happening. Many also thought that the Archbishop was right in dismissing me because I was encouraging unrest and propounding heretical views, but no one ever told me what the heretical views were.

I alternated between moods of anger and anxiety. Part of me wanted to be thoroughly indiscreet about the damage we can do as clergy in the name of Christ, seemingly engendering a Christless Catholicism, laying heavy burdens on people's backs, especially in sexual morality, and lifting not a finger to help them, nurturing bigotry and prejudice in the name of Christ's gospel, making 'Thou shalt not rock the boat' the first and greatest commandment. I began to read the Old Testament prophets with new eyes. But there was another voice which said, 'What about the beam in your own eye? Are you really being honest, or are you so profoundly selfish and obstinate that you have grown blind and can no longer see the damage you are doing?' 'I don't think you know who you are.' Then the anxiety began, because there was truth in this voice, but I also knew that it was not the whole truth. If I were to accept and agree with this voice, it would rob me of any self-trust. I would have to stop searching, questioning, and rely on only one certainty, my own profound weakness, and become an unquestioning, conforming priest.

I was encouraged because so many people supported and helped me, but I still felt confused, uncertain and helpless. I prayed and began to realize how helpless I really was. Out of this came certainty and every Mass I celebrated confirmed it – that God's goodness is far more powerful than our weakness and that he gives himself to us.

Life was much calmer after 1972, but I was beginning to feel the need for time to study and reflect on what I had experienced. I told the Jesuit provincial that I wanted a change and also asked if I could have a year off for study before starting on different work. When I told a priest friend that I was having a year off, his immediate reply was, 'You're not leaving the priesthood, are you?' While the Glasgow experience had forced me to question my faith, the meaning of the Church and the priesthood, this questioning had at the same time deepened my faith in Christ and strengthened my love for the priesthood and the Church.

I looked around for possible courses of study during my sabbatical year. I thought of a counselling course, but was told that if I wanted to do it thoroughly I should spend six years on it and do a doctorate. Then there was the offer of an M. Theol. at an American university with courses in theology and spirituality ancient and modern, all included in a one-year course. One look at the prospectus brought back memories of years of lectures in pre-Vatican II theology which have now left me incapable of listening to the human voice for more than twenty minutes without falling asleep. I shall never have need of sleeping pills; a tape recorder with a theology lecture (the meaning doesn't matter if it's only idle chatter of a transcendental kind) is far more effective and less damaging to health. The M. Theol. prospectus cured me of looking for study courses.

I wanted to study out of my own experience, especially the experience of the last eight years, the experience of conflict within myself and of the conflicts of so many other people, who had given me their confidence. How do I know what God's will really is? How do I discern, sift my own experience, separate out the true from the false, so that I can become more true, more at one with God, with myself, with all creation? 'I don't think you know who you are' re-echoed in my mind, but I did want to search and I decided to study spirituality.

2

Isle of the Sea

There is a story told that the Jesuits of Farm Street, London, once invited the famous Frederick William Faber to preach a panegyric in their church for the feast of St Ignatius of Loyola, the sixteenth-century founder of the Jesuits. For an hour Faber preached with great eloquence, praising the spirituality of Ignatius. Then came his final sentence: 'This, my dear brethren, is St Ignatius' way to heaven; and thank God it is not the only way.'

Some would deny that St Ignatius' spirituality, expressed in a dry little book *The Spiritual Exercises*, is even a possible way to heaven. The sixteenth-century Spanish Inquisition was unhappy about the book and it has had its critics ever since. Ignatius himself describes the Spiritual Exercises as being 'every way of preparing and disposing the soul to rid itself of all disordered attachments, and after their removal, of seeking and finding the will of God in the disposition of our lives for the salvation of our soul.' They are exercises in discernment, in the sifting of our experience, especially our moods, which he calls 'the spirits', in order to discover God's will for us.

As a Jesuit, I had often made the Spiritual Exercises and had given them to others, mostly to members of religious orders, but my Glasgow experience had made me increasingly sceptical about their value. I had heard the Exercises being given both in retreats and, in more diluted form, in sermons and instructions. In many cases they seemed to me to be exercises in blind ecclesiastical conformity rather than in sensitive perception and responsiveness. They were frequently presented as a kind of spiritual strait-jacket. 'Here are the

Spiritual Exercises of St Ignatius, whose value is beyond questioning. They have inspired thousands of Christian men and women, many of them canonized saints and martyrs, and they are still a most valuable instrument for renewal within the Church. Follow them rigorously and you, too, will be renewed and inspired.' Then came the Exercises themselves with their meditations on sin, death, judgement, hell. In the hell meditation he writes, 'Imagine the vast fires, and the souls enclosed, as it were, in bodies of fire.' We are all afraid of life, but even more afraid of what is likely to happen to us after death. To intensify this fear and then present people with an escape route from their terror is an ancient technique for winning power over them.

The Exercises can be given in this way. James Joyce, in his *Portrait of the Artist as a Young Man*, gives a classic description when he describes a Jesuit retreat given to him when he was a schoolboy. Joyce rejected the Exercises given in this way, but others accepted them and became papal shock troops, 'Theirs not to reason why, theirs but to do and die.' Off they have gone, ready to advance under withering fire. I have seen some of the papal shock troops in action – sincere and dedicated men, but unreflective, afraid to think for themselves and suspicious of anyone who does – leaving a trail of pain and havoc in the lives of those unfortunate enough to come under their influence. In the retreats I had given, I had met Religious, broken people, who when asked if they had never discussed their problems before, said, 'Oh yes, but we were always told that fidelity to God means following the third mode of humility.'

In the course of the Exercises Ignatius describes three kinds of humility, the third of which is only possible for a person who is so at one with God and Christ that he can sincerely say, 'I desire and choose poverty with Christ poor rather than riches; insults with Christ loaded with them rather than honours; I desire to be accounted worthless and a fool for Christ rather than to be esteemed as wise and prudent in this world.' To force this ideal on someone, in fact to force any ideal on anyone before they are ready for it, is to destroy them. The Exercises are meant to set us free, not imprison

us in our own morbid fears. In all the counselling I had done
I could see that fear was the root problem in the spiritual life
of very many people. They felt drawn to God in the depths
of themselves, but in the attraction there was also an unac-
knowledged repulsion, which stifled their spiritual growth.
When sifted out in conversation, the repulsion was a hidden
resentment against a God who would not let them be. To
them he was God the lawgiver, God the judge, a monster God.
Until this basic resentment was acknowledged and expressed,
there could be no genuine progress in spiritual development.
The Exercises, given in strait-jacket, Joycian form, far from
liberating, could cripple the retreatant, imprison the spirit
and produce religious nausea, not love of God

I knew that this was not what Ignatius intended and I knew
that much scholarly work had been done on the Exercises,
especially in the last fifty years, but I had only read bits and
pieces, enough to make me want to study more. I began to
do some preliminary reading in the summer of 1974. I
discovered that in Ignatius' own lifetime neither he, nor any
of the early Jesuits, ever gave the Spiritual Exercises to groups
but only to individuals, because, as one of them wrote,
'different individuals have different needs', a basic principle
in spirituality and in every form of education. When it is
ignored, the most sublime spirituality can become destructive.
Before giving someone the Exercises, the early Jesuits would
spend a long time getting to know their retreatants. Ignatius
himself lived for years with two of his first companions,
Francis Xavier and Peter Favre, before he gave them the
Exercises.

I began to read the familiar text of the Exercises with
closer attention. The book begins with a few preliminary
observations. The second observation cautions the director
against talking too much. He must present the matter factu-
ally and briefly. 'It is not much knowledge which fills and
satisfies the soul,' writes Ignatius, 'but the intimate understanding and relish of the truth.' The retreatant is to be
allowed to make discoveries for himself out of his own experience. In a later observation Ignatius further describes the role
of the director. He must not persuade the retreatant to one

course of action rather than another, but, 'as a balance at equilibrium, without leaning to one side or the other, he should permit the creature to deal directly with his Creator and Lord'.

How does God deal directly with us? Does he only deal with us by presenting us with his laws and doctrines, giving them to us through his Church? Are we to try and understand the laws and doctrines as far as we can and then, by an act of the will, assent to them, encouraged in our assent by the fear of what will happen to us if we do not? God does not treat us in this impersonal, abstract fashion. He is not the God of the philosophers, but the God of Abraham, Isaac and Jacob, the God who dispossessed himself and became incarnate in Christ, in whom we live and move and have our being. He speaks to us in the depths of our being, not off the top of our heads. The depths of ourselves are not in our reasoning and in our ideas, still less in someone else's reasoning and ideas. If we are to find God, we must learn to listen to these depths, to the emotions and feelings which we experience in prayer and out of it, and use our minds and intelligence to help us understand what these emotions and feelings are saying to us. To make the Spiritual Exercises as will-strengthening exercises to help us conform to ready-made ideas and doctrines, however sublime in themselves, is like trying to grow physically strong and healthy by reading books on body-building and dietetics without taking exercises or meals.

It was because Ignatius considered moods and their interpretation ('discernment of spirits') so important as an indication of God's will for us, that he always gave the Exercises to individuals. Each day the retreatant would meet with his director and talk about the moods he had experienced in prayer. By beginning to put our feelings into words we become more in touch with them and can begin to understand them better. The director's function is not to interpret the moods for the retreatant, but to help him learn to discern for himself. This is a totally different method of retreat-giving from the methods which I had felt uneasy about. The Inquisitors knew how the Exercises were originally given. That is why they were uneasy about them.

A number of Glasgow students had been asking for a serious retreat. I offered them one of eight days in August 1974, limiting the number to a maximum of eight and giving it in the manner, in so far as I knew it, in which the Exercises were originally given.

Before giving the retreat to students, I decided to make one myself and looked around for a place where I could be sure of solitude and freedom from all distractions. I had decided to go to a Cistercian monastery when I met, by chance, an old friend, Father David Lake, an Anglican priest, who had been assistant chaplain at Glasgow University a few years before. He was looking very sunburned and windswept and told me that he had just returned from Eileach an Naoimh, a desert island off the west coast of Scotland, where he lived for three weeks. Eileach an Naoimh means 'the rocky islet of the saints' and lies to the south of Mull about 24 kilometres from Iona, the island where St Columba settled and from which Scotland was evangelized. According to legend, St Brendan had lived on Eileach an Naoimh, St Columba retired to it whenever Iona became too much for him and the Princess Eithne, Columba's mother, is said to lie buried on a hillock on the island. Whatever the truth in the legends, there was certainly a small monastic settlement on the island. The walls of a ninth-century Celtic chapel are still standing and also the ruins of two interconnected beehive cells. Near the chapel there is a curious underground cell, known as the dungeon, which provides the only sheltered spot on the island. This sounded an ideal spot for a retreat, so I arranged with a fisherman to take me over, borrowed some camping equipment and did some hurried shopping, a hurry I was later to regret.

It was a clear day with a fresh wind and choppy sea when I left the mainland in an open boat to sail to the island. An hour later I was landed on the rocks of Eileach an Naoimh, a moment I shall never forget. I sat on the rock ledge in the rain watching the boat return to the mainland with my sister and two friends. On the ledge beside me were my possessions:

21

a tent, sleeping bag, rucksack and cardboard box marked
'dog biscuits'. For a few moments I cursed myself for my
sudden enthusiasm which I so often regret later, but the
survival instinct was stronger than self-recrimination. I took
hold of the sodden dog-biscuit box and clambered over the
rocks in search of the underground cell. The rocks gave way
to swampy ground and then I saw the fence enclosing the
monastery ruins with the Celtic chapel walls still standing to
a height of about two metres on the east side.

A few metres in front of the south wall of the chapel there
was a hole in the ground giving entry to the underground
cell. Worn steps curved down to a flat circular space paved
with stones which was about 2 metres below ground. On the
left hand side of this open space there was a small entrance
to the cell, whose floor was a metre below the level of the
open circle. I reversed into the cell which was circular in
shape, paved with stones and about a metre in diametre. The
moss-covered walls, formed by smooth stones laid horizon-
tally, curved upwards to the apex a metre above the floor. I
dragged the dog-biscuit box inside and returned to the rocks
to collect the rest of my equipment.

Then I began to search for the well. The boatman who
had brought me across was a stranger to the island and did
not know where the well was, but he assured me that it
would not be difficult to find. After ten minutes searching my
confidence was ebbing; after twenty minutes I was speculating
how long it would take before thirst became an agony, and
after half an hour how long the agony would last before death.
Suddenly I found it, a small stream trickling out of a rock
near the shore. It formed a little basin, surrounded by rock
plants and flowers; later this became my refrigerator. I set
up the tent and then began to explore the island.

Eileach an Naoimh is the southernmost of a group of islands
known as the Gavellachs or 'isle of the sea', which lie in the
mouth of the Firth of Lorne, between Mull to the north
and Scarba to the south. The islands are uninhabited and
inaccessible, not because of their remoteness (they are only
11 kilometres from the mainland), but because they are
exposed to the full force of the Atlantic gales which sweep up

from the west. The huge seas breaking on the rocky shores make landing difficult. The island itself is about 2 kilometres long and 400 metres wide. Low on the eastern side, it rises to the west and then drops sheer into the Atlantic with cliffs 74 metres high. In formation it is as though huge slabs of rock had been hurled in turn against the high, vertical wall of rock on the west side, each slab slightly lower than the one it leans against. Although called 'the rocky islet' there are little valleys running the length of the island between the rock slabs, rich in grass and wild flowers. The mainland farmers often use the island for sheep grazing.

Even on that first grey evening the view from the top of the island was astonishingly beautiful. To the north-east was the opening to the great glen of Scotland; to the north and north-west the mountains and mainland of Mull; to the south the open sea and the outline of the islands of Colonsay and Jura, and to the east the mountains of the mainland. I walked the length of the island along the cliff top with the gulls wheeling and crying overhead, ending at the unmanned lighthouse at the southern tip. I felt no fear at being alone. The island was peaceful and friendly. That evening, when the wind had dropped and the sky cleared, I slept with the tent open facing the sea. I wanted to be able to watch the night sky, hear the roar of the sea, listen to the gulls and watch the dawn breaking. I fell asleep quickly and it was well after dawn when I awoke, my sleeping bag half out of the tent and soaking wet. I washed at the well and prepared breakfast, ready for a damp day.

As I sat on one of the steps leading to the underground cell in a gloom which matched the damp mist, I tried to prepare myself for the retreat I had come to make. Then the mist began to rise, the sun broke through and within half an hour the whole island was transformed. The grey sea became a lovely blue flecked with white, the morning sun touched the island with its rays revealing it in all its beauty: the rich green valleys running between the brown rock, the rock crevasses dotted with an astonishing variety of wild flowers. I sat and watched.

Sitting, watching, gazing became the pattern of my days.

The beauty and the peace of this lovely isle began to take hold of me, still me, teach me. It was like an inner cleansing of the mind and senses. I began to notice simple things, the rocks, the stones, the shells, the wild flowers, the birds and gulls as though I were seeing them for the first time, and I never grew tired of looking. It was the same with spiritual truths. If I put into words the things I learned, I write platitudes and clichés, but the island, and later the walk to Rome, taught me the value of platitudes.

Silence, I had always known, is helpful for prayer, and I used to try to keep silence in retreats, but keeping silence can be a noisy business and does not necessarily still the spirit. The island silence was of a different kind. I did not 'practise' silence; it took hold of me. Prayer became much less of an exercise and more of a repose. God is everywhere and God is mystery. I already knew that was true, but on the island there was the space and time to relish the truth, to be seized and permeated by it. Being alone on this tiny islet of the sea, I was forced to meditate on the tininess, insignificance and precariousness of my existence. Our own world is a speck in the vast universe, this island did not even merit a dot on most maps. These rocks were formed millions of years ago and here was I sitting on them, an ant-like creature, a very recent newcomer to life for all my fifty years, passing through life fleetingly on my way to death.

These thoughts did not lead me to feelings of hopelessness and despair, but to a sense of helplessness and wonder, to a sense of abandonment to life and gratitude for it. I realised how little control I had over my own life and destiny. I did not engineer my birth, I have hardly begun to know how my body works, my brain cells, my breathing. Life is a gift. As this knowledge dawned on me, I began to experience a curious affinity with the island, with its rocks and wild flowers, with its birds and gulls, and I was not afraid. 'Man lasts no longer than grass,' says the psalmist, 'no longer than a wild flower he lives: one gust of wind, and he is gone, never to be seen there again; yet Yahweh's love for those who fear him lasts from all eternity and forever.'

On my second evening on the island I celebrated Mass in

24

the ancient Celtic chapel, using an upturned fish box for an altar. Normally, a priest should not celebrate Mass alone, because Mass is not a private devotion, but a communal act of worship. But on the island I had no scruple. I read the Scriptures aloud to the sheep and the gulls and to all creation. The bread and wine I offered were symbols of my own life, of the lives of all my friends and relatives, of all human life. And over the bread I said the words of Christ, 'This is my body, given for you.' It is the whole of creation which is mysteriously being transformed, every particle of it. 'Take and eat.' The mysterious God, God of majesty and power, in whom all creation has its being, has spoken to us in Christ, is still with us in every instant of our existence and speaks his love for us in this most wonderful sign. 'Do this in memory of me' does not simply mean 'continue to celebrate the Eucharist'; it also says, 'your life, too, must be given for others'. I wondered when Mass had first been celebrated on that island and when the last Mass had been said. In this Mass I felt at one with the first and the last.

St Ignatius divided his Exercises into four parts, the first being a series of meditations on sin. He expected the retreatant in making the Exercises to experience changes of mood and feeling. He divided the moods into two categories, which he called 'consolation' and 'desolation'. 'I call consolation every increase of faith, hope and love, and all interior joy that invites and attracts to what is heavenly and to the salvation of one's soul by filling it with peace and quiet in its Creator and Lord. I call desolation what is entirely the opposite – darkness of soul, turmoil of spirit, inclination to what is low and earthly, restlessness arising from many disturbances and temptations, which lead to want of faith, want of hope, want of love.' It was through discernment of these moods that he believed we could begin to learn God's will for us.

I had always disliked this first part of the Exercises, not only because the 'consideration and contemplation of sin' is a morbid subject in itself, but because I had seen so many lives broken by religious introspection and fear, drained of their humanity, leaving cold and lifeless people whose main preoccupation is to avoid doing anything wrong. I disliked, too, the selectiveness of so much Catholic moral teaching on the nature of sin – failing to attend Mass on Sundays and holy days of obligation, any wilful sexual pleasure outside marriage, failing to assent to the teaching of the Catholic Church and to support its pastors. Truthfulness, honesty, integrity, justice both private and public, were less frequently emphasized. I shall always remember a conversation with a student, a talented and generous girl, whose life was dominated by religious fear and scruples. I asked her once, 'If you can imagine yourself totally free without any rules or regulations to observe, what would you most like to do?' 'Burn down churches,' was her shattering reply.

I never began on the meditations on sin; they began in me. I set aside time each day for formal prayer, praying at first not from a scripture text but from the vision of creation all around me. The Spiritual Exercises end with a 'Contemplation to attain the love of God'. In it Ignatius instructs the retreatant, 'I will ponder with great affection how much God our Lord has done for me, and how much he has given me of what he possesses, and finally how much, as far as he can, the same Lord desires to give himself to me . . . Reflect how God dwells in creatures, in the elements giving them existence, in the plants giving them life, in the animals conferring on them sensation; so he dwells in me and gives me being, life, sensation, intelligence, and makes a temple of me, since I am created in the likeness and image of the divine majesty.' Thoughts from this contemplation passed through my mind as I looked at the sea and the sky, the plants and the animals. The truth was overwhelming, like waves breaking over me, sweeping me out of myself and leaving me speechless.

Prayer is so different from thinking. Thinking is like preparing the route before climbing a mountain; praying is the climb itself, a totally different experience.

I sat looking out over the sea. What is it all saying, all that I see and feel, hear and touch, taste and smell, imagine and remember, conceive of and long for? St Paul says of Christ, 'He is the image of the unseen God'. Christ is the mysterious God translated into human terms, 'something', as St John says in his first letter, 'which has existed since the beginning, that we have heard, and we have seen with out own eyes, that we have watched and touched with our hands; the Lord who is life'. God is everywhere, God is good, God is love. 'It is not much knowledge which fills and satisfies the soul, but the intimate understanding and relish of the truth.' It was while this truth of God's goodness was breaking in on me that I also began to see my own sinfulness, my own refusal to believe in his goodness, to let him be the God of love, preferring a more impersonal God.

I remembered a phrase from thirty years before. In the noviciate we were given lessons in preaching a model sermon, expressed in very Victorian English. It began, 'As pride was the first sin, so it is the source and origin of all the sins that are committed.' We had to practise this set piece with suitable gestures and inflections of the voice. It never failed to raise a laugh. One novice was so expansive in his gestures that he shattered the light bulb over his right shoulder. We were so intent on gestures and modulation of the voice that most of us never gave a thought to the content. Now I saw the truth of it so clearly. Pride means not letting God be God, not really believing in his goodness, not entrusting ourselves to it, not recognising his goodness at work in us. Instead we create a God after our own image and likeness and then condemn everyone who is not like us. Sin is forgetfulness of his goodness. Ignatius has a prayer at the end of one of his meditations on sin, 'This is a cry of wonder accompanied by surging emotion as I pass in review all creatures. How is it that they have permitted me to live, and have sustained me in life! Why have the angels, though they are the sword of God's justice, tolerated me, guarded me and prayed for me! – and the heavens, sun, moon, stars, and the elements; the fruits, birds, fishes and other animals – why have they all been at my service!'

The meditations on sin were not exercises in gloom and morbid introspection. They were an experience of peace and reconciliation within myself. Inhibited creature that I am, I found myself singing 'Gloria Dei', flinging my arms out to

27

catch all creation, talking to the moon and the stars, the gulls and the sheep.

I spent eight days on the island. I knew the euphoria could not last, but I was not worried. The goodness and graciousness of God was the anchor of my hope, and nothing could take that away from me. And I knew I must return to this island which had given me such peace.

A few days later I went to Stonyhurst College in Lancashire, where I had arranged to give the retreat to eight students. We had already had some preliminary meetings, so they knew what to expect. I had told them that we would have a half-hour session together each day during which I would suggest methods and material for prayer, but for the rest of the time I would leave them on their own to reflect and pray. I would also see each of them individually every day, if they wanted to come. I told them, too, that the object of this interview was to discuss how they felt during the meditations rather than what they thought, because it is through these feelings that we can begin to discern what God is asking of us. I was apprehensive in case the Exercises would not 'take', in case the retreatants grew bored and restless and felt they were wasting their time. I had misjudged the power of the Exercises, which soon engaged them. As I listened to them every day and to their honest description of their own feelings, I began to see more clearly that the Exercises really are a way of finding God, even if not the only way, and the pity is that so far, in England, they are rarely given to the laity in the manner Ignatius gave them.

I had already decided to go to Rome for part of my sabbatical year to do some study on Ignatian spirituality. One wet afternoon at Stonyhurst, when I was feeling too sluggish to stir from my chair and go for a walk, the thought came to me, 'why not walk to Rome?' I mentioned the idea to someone and was told soon afterwards, 'I hear you are walking to Rome: what a splendid idea!' Then it became, 'I hear you are making a pilgrimage on foot to Rome for the Holy Year.' These were pious thoughts, which had not even occurred to me at first.

I decided to walk to Rome, not only because I wanted to

study there and have always liked walking, but because I wanted to try to recapture and deepen the island experience. St Ignatius used to call himself 'the pilgrim' and went on pilgrimage to Jerusalem after his conversion. Later he insisted that candidates for the Society of Jesus should go on pilgrimage for a month. I wanted to understand more about his Exercises and hoped that the pilgrimage might help me to understand more of his spirituality.

3

Cliffs of Fall

Between August 1974, when I decided to walk to Rome, and April 1975, when I left the Glasgow chaplaincy, I had very little time to make any detailed preparations.

One day in January 1975, the Catholic Press Office rang up to ask me what I intended doing when I left Glasgow. I told them I was walking to Rome to study there. The Catholic newspaper, *The Universe*, carried a short paragraph in its next number, and this brought me three interesting letters.

The first letter was from a man in the south of England warning me against the undertaking. He had spent many years living in Europe, including Rome. The medieval pilgrim, he wrote, risked the hazards of encountering beasts and brigands, warring armies, floods and disease, but these were as nothing compared with today's dangers of death from Fiat, Renault and Peugeot. He advised me to find some cheap form of travel and see the treasures of Christian Europe at leisure!

The second letter was much more encouraging. It was from an Edinburgh man, Ian Tweedie, who had walked to Rome from Aldershot a few years before, taking fifty-three days for the journey. Ian had been in the army and, like Hilaire Belloc who immortalized his walk in *The Path to Rome*, he began from the spot 'where he had served in arms for his sins'. Ian now lectures in engineering and had applied his skills to construct a little trolley, which he used to draw his rucksack behind him across France, over the Great St Bernard Pass and down to Rome. He sent me a copy of his diary of the trip with its terse descriptions of each day. 'Had plums for breakfast and walked ten kms before stopping for coffee. Found cemetery

for night. Head down 9.30.' He invited me over to his Edinburgh home where he had laid out all his equipment,
including a rucksack filled with water bottles to give me some
idea of the weight I would have to carry. I still remember
how I staggered as I put on his rucksack and began the
traverse of his sitting room. Ian could not have been more
helpful; he warned me of the importance of travelling light
and offered to construct a trolley for me if I showed him my
haversack. He even confessed that his first thought had been
not a trolley, but a pram.

Ian's letter was followed by news from another Rome
walker, Edwin Unsworth from Manchester. When already in
his sixties he had walked from Manchester to Rome. He, too,
sent me his diaries which I found very encouraging. If a man
in his sixties could do it, there was hope for a youngster in
his fifties.

In March, through a gift of the students, I bought an
orange-coloured nylon frame rucksack, the lightest of the large
ones I could find, and a week later I went off with a group
of twenty students for a week's hill-walking at the start of the
Easter vacation. We stayed at Inverailort Castle, Lochailort,
where the owner, Mrs Cameron Head, kindly gave us shelter.
I had been up to Lochailort regularly since 1968 with student
groups, for conferences in September and for walking in
March.

Normally, we walked cross-country, but this year I
suggested a road walk of about 20 kilometres from Lochailort
to the white sands of Morar, part of the famous 'road to the
isles'. I offered to carry all their food and spare clothing in
the new orange rucksack.

We set off at a great pace on a perfect March day, frosty
but clear. Spring had taken hold of the students who sang
and danced their way, with occasional backward glances to
see how I was managing. I shambled along under the weight
of their sandwiches, leaning slightly forward and feeling like
an under-nourished ape. We had a ten-minute rest every
hour, a practice which Ian Tweedie had recommended and
which I later kept to all the way to Rome, with only a few
exceptions. The road to the isles is a road of surprises as it

31

twists and turns its way through forests and along lochsides until it meets the sea. The view from the hill above Arisaig across to the island of Skye with its snowcapped Cuillins and the islands of Eigg and Rhum, the blue sea and the russet colour of the hills, the singing and dancing which was louder now and more vigorous because we had found a pub just before closing time: all this distracted me from the growing pain in my shoulders, legs and heels.

When we reached the white sands of Morar, some strange masochistic urge seized us all and led us into the March Atlantic. The sea at this time of year has an anaesthetizing effect and we thrashed around for a few seconds, paying for our vanity. It was when my circulation returned that I was able to assess the damages of the walk. My legs were very stiff and I had a large blister on each heel. The stiffness soon wore off and I knew I was strong enough to do the walk to Rome provided I could harden my feet. Everyone in the party had their own piece of advice about footcare. 'Wear cotton socks,' said one. 'There's no substitute for a good thick pair of woollen socks,' said another, who claimed to have walked for five years in the same pair of socks without ever washing them. 'Wash your feet frequently,' said another. 'Don't wash your feet, it only softens them.' 'Bathe them in methylated spirits regularly.' 'Bathe them in methylated spirits and you'll harden the outer skin so that you develop deep, painful blisters inside.' In view of all this conflicting advice I decided that the only safe method was to keep walking and harden the heels naturally.

I left the Glasgow chaplaincy for the last time on Sunday, April 13, after the evening Mass. I could not absorb the fact that I was leaving this place where I had spent the happiest years of my life. The parting was like an amputation, but I did not feel the full pain of it until much later when, returning from Rome to Glasgow, I collected my luggage and moved to London.

As I had various engagements in England and Scotland, I could not set out for Rome until June 19. From Glasgow I went over to visit cousins in Dublin and while there I started to plan the route to Rome. I began with a small-scale map, drawing straight lines between the places I wanted to visit: London, Newhaven, Dieppe, Paris, Vézelay, Taiźe, Grenoble, Siena, Rome. Then I began to work on larger-scale maps, marking out routes which avoided main roads and yet keeping as close as possible to the straight lines. Where the minor roads diverged too much, I drew in dotted lines to indicate a cross-country route. I worked out a time schedule which allowed for 24–32 kilometres each day and a few reserve days for emergencies. I planned to leave London on June 19 and to arrive in Rome on September 8. I laid out all the fourteen maps from London to Rome in the garden one day and was full of confidence that having worked out the route and schedule on paper, the walk itself would be a mere formality.

At the beginning of May I returned to Eileach an Naoimh for two weeks to enjoy its peace, learn Italian, do some reading and toughen myself for the walk. I had told many of my friends about the island and they wanted to come and have a look at it. I phoned the boatman asking him how many people he could take across. 'I'm allowed to drown fourteen at a time,' was his reply. So fourteen of us landed and the visitors had time to scurry over the island before returning to the mainland. As they left the island, escorted by a shoal of seals, I sat watching for a long time after the boat had disappeared beyond the skerries. I felt no fear at being alone nor at the prospect of two weeks solitary confinement. The last eight years had left me with a longing for peace and quiet.

On my first visit to the island the previous August I had shopped hurriedly on the day of my departure. Among other things, I had bought a number of malt loaves and eight tins of Irish stew. After two days I fed the malt loaves to the gulls and eventually returned home with five tins of Irish stew. For breakfast I used to have porridge and discovered the origin of the Scottish habit of taking porridge standing, or walking about. I found myself doing this instinctively in the early morning to keep the circulation going. For the main meal, when I could no longer face Irish stew, I ate the most hideous concoctions of what remained in my supplies: a base of powdered soup with cheese and raisins mixed, followed by rice and raisins. With some fruit and chocolate I found it a healthy diet. On the second visit I was far less spartan and took a variety of tinned foods (excluding Irish stew), with oatmeal biscuits in place of malt loaves. I had no set timetable on the island, but ate when I was hungry and slept when I was tired. I began to discover, both on the island and later on the walk, the difference between GMT and biological time. Towards the end of the two weeks on the island I was eating twice a day, a breakfast about 9 a. m. and a main meal around 8 p. m. Hours of sleep varied, but both on the island and on the walk I needed less sleep than usual and was surprised on a few occasions when I walked all night, that I did not feel particularly tired the next day.

When the boat departed I returned to the enclosure to set up camp. The underground cell, which had been dry in August, was ankle-deep in water and I spent the first hour carrying large flat stones into the cell to provide a dry surface for storing. By the time I had finished my first evening meal I was shivering with cold in spite of two heavy pullovers. I removed one pullover, put on a pair of shorts and gym shoes and began running along the valleys, zigzagging to the island's summit. I was puffing heavily on the gradients, but had a glorious run on the uppermost ridge along the edge of the cliffs, greeted the gulls, the sheep and the lambs and returned to the tent feeling warm at last. I put on all the clothes I had, zipped up the tent and crawled into my sleeping bag. In August I slept on a camp bed in a borrowed tent. This time I had been given a gift of a small lightweight tent for the walk to Rome, too small to take a camp bed, and in its place I had a strip of very light waterproof matting, thick and long enough to cushion me from shoulder to thigh against sharp and hard surfaces. I rested my feet on the haversack laid flat at the end of the tent. After an hour's wriggling I found a comfortable position and slept soundly. The tent was given a good testing on the island in some very stormy weather. It kept out the rain, withstood the wind and, greatest advantage of all, there was no condensation.

This second visit to the island was different from the first.

The weather was much colder in May than in August, the nights were longer, the winds stronger and the storms fiercer. At times, too, my spirit matched the weather. However, apart from a few stormy days, the sky was bright and clear and the sun felt warm when I could find a spot sheltered from the wind. I had not come to make the Spiritual Exercises this time, but for a period of peace and quiet. Apart from my Italian lessons and reading I wanted to do some regular running to make myself stronger and to walk barefoot on the rocks to harden my feet.

When I return to the island again I shall take no books, no transistor, no agenda of my own, but let it teach me its own lessons as on the first occasion. For the first fews days I was very busy, but then my plans began to crumble and finally collapsed. I soon gave up the barefoot walking after I had collected a few thorns and I abandoned the running partly through laziness but also because I was afraid of pulling a muscle or twisting an ankle on the uneven surfaces. My transistor batteries died, fortunately, and I decided that the Italian lessons could wait. When I stopped trying to organize myself, the island's peace began to take hold of me again.

I said Mass each day in the Celtic chapel. The fish box which I had used as an altar had disappeared, but I found it later down by the sea edge and carried it back again. My thoughts, both during the Mass and afterwards, kept returning to those Celtic monks who had lived on the island, celebrated this same Mass on it and now lay buried there. I knew little of the Celtic Church and had to rely on my imagination. I could imagine their physical appearance, tough weather-beaten men, but how did they think, what kind of theology drove them to live out their lives on this remote island?

I had read of the terrifying asceticism of the early Irish monks. Was it fear of 'the world' which drove them to this remote island where they could endure the hardships of wild weather and hunger and add other mortifications to their heart's content? Did they deliberately build their doorways so low, forcing them to stoop on entering, because they felt

35

that the harder life is, the more pleasing it is to God, an idea which still survives in many forms of spirituality today? Did they live here because, as I once heard a monk express it, 'It's a hard bed to lie on, but a sweet bed to die on'? Had they built the underground cell as a punishment place for recalcitrant monks, as at least one writer has suggested?

The island did not feel as though it had been populated with hard-faced, gloomy ascetics, preoccupied with their own and other people's sinfulness; haters of the body, whose main interest was in subduing it and extracting from it the suffering which they thought God was demanding as the price of their sinfulness, a price to be paid either here or, more painfully, hereafter. To me the island was a peaceful place, a holy place: I never felt lonely on it. I wanted to believe that the first monks had settled there, not because it was barren and rugged, but because it was beautiful; that they landed one day in their coracle, found the well and then climbed to the western heights. There they saw the beauty and grandeur of the island and felt compelled to stay. I wanted to believe their ascetic practices were never done for their own sake, or from belief in an avenging God, but that God had touched them, given them a new awareness of his goodness which they never wanted to lose, and that all their ascetic practices were their attempts to keep alive in themselves this sense of his presence.

One day the previous August when it had poured with rain all day and my tent was thoroughly soaked, I spent most of the day huddled inside the little underground cell. By the end of the day I knew why they had built it. I sat crouched in a kind of womb position in the semi-darkness surrounded by these ancient stones, formed millions of years ago, and in this darkness and restriction I glimpsed the path to freedom.

As I sat there, I tried to distract my mind from the discomfort I was feeling, remembering the night before when I sat at the top of the island watching the sunset, the moon appearing towards the east in the night sky. 'In him all created things have their being.' 'Do not be afraid, for I have redeemed you; I have called you by name, you are mine.' I remembered the waves of wonder, the exhilaration I had felt, but soreness and damp brought me back to the reality of this cramped little cell and I thought of that other cave, the cave of Bethlehem. God, who holds the vast universe in being, God of all times and of all ages, presents himself to us as this whimpering child lying in an animal's feeding trough, a God in need, a helpless God, who needs man's help and protection. 'His weakness is stronger than human strength; his folly wiser than human wisdom,' wrote St Paul. Israel had boasted, 'There is no God as great as our God,' but his greatness is in his power to love and to become the least of all. God was as present in the restriction of this little cell as he was in the heavens. No thing, no person is too small for him. I knew why they had built this little cell. It was a place for prayer.

All asceticism is, or should be, to deepen our awareness of this truth: that God is love, the incredibly gentle, tender, gracious and generous God, Emmanuel, God within us and among us. Everything in the Church, her doctrines, discipline, liturgy, organization is a means to an end, to open us up to the goodness of God, to make us more and more sensitive and perceptive to his presence within each of us. Perceiving this presence with all our being, we want to respond to it. That is the theory: the practice is often so different. We can bury God under a heap of doctrinal formulations and tell people that they can only find God if they assent to these formulations. We can hide the gentle self-giving of Christ under the sign of bread and wine by celebrating it in such an impersonal way that his guests can no longer recognize it as a sign of love, or by hedging it about with so many theological explanations and warnings that they are afraid to approach. I often heard students say, 'I don't go to Mass any more because I don't believe in transubstantiation.'

It was not all peace on the island. There were stormy moments, too. How real was this experience of God's goodness? How far was I running away from real experience and vaporising in pious thoughts, floating around in a fantasy world, which would disappear when I returned to the mainland? I sometimes dream that I can float on air and wonder to myself in sleep, 'Why did I never do this before? It's so simple.' Perhaps the island experience was like my dreams. But at another level I knew that these glimpses of God's goodness were glimpses of reality. They made me feel whole and at one, or rather they showed me the possibility of being whole and at one, because the glimpses also showed me the shallowness of my faith and the depths of disbelief and distrust that were in me. But self-knowledge in the light of his goodness is bearable. He first loved me, and he is faithful. A phrase of Julian of Norwich was often in my mind: 'All will be well, all will be well, all manner of things will be well.'

This reassuring phrase did not prevent me from thinking about things that were not well and from complaining about them in prayer. I thought about Christ the baby, Christ the lost child, Christ of the Sermon on the Mount, Christ of the homely parables, Christ who had pity on the crowds, Christ crucified in the name of law, order and religion. I also thought about some recent events in which Christ was presented to people as the forbidding legalist, and I became angry.

I thought of student Masses at Lochailort. We used to celebrate the Mass in the dining-room. Students prepared the liturgy with great care and endless discussion. They were surprised to learn that the Mass could be enjoyable, that it was showing them a new dimension in their lives, especially in their relations to each other. The Mass had come alive and they recognized Christ in the breaking of bread. He was the bond of their love and peace. One evening they broke into spontaneous dance at the end of it. Yet these Masses, for all their informality, were celebrated prayerfully and with reverence. Later, we were forbidden to celebrate Mass in this way. We had to go to the chapel, which was cold and uncomfortable, where they sat shivering in serried ranks while something died in them. All this was done in the name of 'reverence, otherwise you don't know where it will end'.

During the Mass, before communion, the priest wishes the people 'the Peace of Christ'. In earlier centuries Christians used to turn and greet each other at this point, but the tradition had died until the Second Vatican Council revived it. When I first introduced it in the chaplaincy at Glasgow, a woman approached me at the end and said, 'I didn't like your Mass.' 'What was it you disliked in the Mass?' I asked. 'That handshaking,' she said. 'You never know what dirty, grimy, filthy hand you are going to have to shake.' There was a whole false theology in that remark, as though God descended vertically on each respectable head at Mass, filled it up with divine grace and the assurance of protection from all contact with dirty people, a God of cleanliness and respectability. One bishop legislated that in his diocese the peace of Christ might be given, but without any physical contact! I know these are trivial examples, but they are symptoms of something much more serious, the refusal to let God be the God who took flesh and lived with us.

'There was no room for them in the inn.' Today, there is often no room for him in the home, especially in the broken home, in the urban jungle home, in the anxious, bewildered, disillusioned heart. There was no room for him in many of the student flats where they were searching in their own rather boozy way for a meaning to their lives; bored with conventional Catholicism as they had encountered it, wanting to question but being told that they were getting above themselves, meeting not with sympathy but with condemnation. They went searching in the '60s and early '70s, trying a little bit of transcendental meditation with a little bit of 'pot', feeling deperately lonely, sleeping around with each other and growing increasingly unhappy. They were condemned for their immorality when so many of them were in search of a morality, a meaning for their lives, some inspiration and an example from their elders who, indulging in the more acceptable drugs of alcohol and tranquillisers, sometimes threw up their hands in horror and told them to get back to Mass and the sacraments.

'All will be well, all will be well, all manner of things will be well.' 'All very well,' I argued with the Lord, 'but look what is happening in your Church. The majority of people are totally disinterested; and can you blame them? Church to them means regular church-going, and they'll have none of it. It does not speak to them, has nothing to offer them except guilt and condemnation. Don't you care that this is happening? Why do you let us priests, religious men and women, go on taking vows, living a "religious life", writing books, going to conferences, pouring out platitudes at each other in our efforts at "renewal", deploring the materialism of our times and preaching against it, while we sit materially secure, untouched by the desperation and disbelief of the people we claim to serve?'

'Lord, shake our security, plunge us into poverty, material and spiritual, make us powerless so that we can enter into lives and let men know that you are the gentle, patient, suffering God, who is risen again.' I grew afraid of my own growing restlessness and of the anger which was taking hold of me. I know so many people, far better Christians than I, who do not appear to experience this restlessness and anger. What kind of spirit was leading me? Among the books I had brought to the island was a collection of Gerard Manley Hopkin's poems. I had often read his black sonnets. Now as I sat on the cliff top above the grey sea, I felt I knew something of this darkness when he wrote,

> O the mind, mind has mountains, cliffs of fall
> Frightful, sheer, no man fathomed.

Far greater than my fear of restlessness and anger was fear of its opposite. I was afraid of anaesthetizing these feelings, of refusing to acknowledge these 'cliffs of fall', of becoming a 'damned good religious' and dying before death.

But the two weeks were not wholly spent in anguish and anger. Underlying the restlessness there was a conviction of God's unbelievable, unpredictable, immeasurable goodness. And there were comforting thoughts, too, about the Church. I thought of the Little Sisters of Jesus whom I had met. They were refined, educated French women living in the top flat of a council house on a desolate Glasgow housing estate. One of them worked in a factory making boiler suits, another was in a shirt factory and the third kept house. A few months after their arrival the local lads paid them their greatest compliment and sprayed outside the entrance to their flat, 'Nuns O.K.' I thought of so many other people across the Christian denominations and outside them, who faced appalling crises and constant hard work, yet they never seemed to lose their serenity and could infect others with their peace.

For all my grumbles and complaints, I was grateful to the Catholic Church and within it to the Society of Jesus which had given me so much.

During my two weeks on the island, my only contact with another human being was on a very wet and stormy day when I saw a fishing boat approaching. I donned oilskins and wellingtons and went down to the edge of the rocks, hoping to meet visitors. The boat came within 50 metres and a voice shouted, 'Are you all right?' 'Yes,' I said, 'where are you from?' But before I could hear a reply the boat had turned and headed out to sea again.

It was a bright, clear day when the boatman came to collect me after two weeks on the island. The seals were there to escort us out beyond the skerries and then we headed north-east to the mainland. I have read of the effects of LSD, how it intensifies the perceptions, especially colour. I felt something of this on leaving the island, a delight in everything around me and a feeling of peace.

A few days after my return I set off again, this time to do a week's walking in the highlands, carrying all the equipment I would need for the Rome walk. The rucksack weighed 17 kilos. I chose a cross-country route, starting at Dunoon on the north side of the Firth of Clyde and planned to go to Oban, Ballachulish, cross over by ferry to the Ardnamurchan peninsula and walk out to the lighthouse, the most westerly point of Britain, returning across the north side of the peninsula and ending the walk at Lochailort. The weather in this last week of May was exceptional for Scotland. There was not a drop of rain, clear skies all day and what I then considered a very hot sun.

I started walking from Dunoon and headed north along the Holy Loch, which looked so still and peaceful and deserving of its name. Yet this is the loch which harbours the Polaris submarines, those demonic beasts which move silently beneath the waters and can emerge, strike, obliterate a people and devastate their land. The loch looked so still, smiling in the sun, but under the surface lurked a destructive power, power to tear human flesh and burn it, torture it, maim it, deform it for generations, even exterminate it. 'God bless this ship and all who sail in her.' What blasphemy! Yes, there

41

had been protest marches and sit-ins, exorcisms even, but people had grown tired and disillusioned when they saw the futility of their protests.

It was not only the Holy Loch which harboured destructive weaponry. 'By yon bonnie banks and by yon bonnie braes, where the sun shines bright on Loch Lomond' there lies the highest concentration of nuclear arms in Europe. We hear about this, but we allow ourselves to forget it, anaesthetize our fears and soothe our uneasy minds with empty phrases about self-defence and deterrents which guarantee peace to all men.

The evil does not lie beneath the waters of the Holy Loch or under the hills of Loch Lomond. It lies within our human hearts: nice, respectable, even religiously minded hearts. We become so out of touch with ourselves that we cannot see that these weapons protect nothing, that they are here and now as destructive to ourselves as they could be in the future to the enemy. Many of the mentally ill people I have met are very imaginative. They cannot bear the pain of life, because they are more sensitive, more human than the rest of us. The only way to survive is to anaesthetize feelings and imagination.

It was at this point in my thinking that I reached the 'cliffs of fall' again. I realized that only part of me was horrified, that I could dismiss these thoughts from my mind, benumb my feelings, function 'normally', be accepted as a balanced, prudent man and so die before death. I prayed to God to save me from all false security, from the false gods of 'reasonableness' and 'common sense', to create a heart of flesh in me and save me from death of imagination and human feeling. 'What does it profit a man if he gains the whole world and suffers the loss of his own soul?' 'The whole world' includes reputation, security of mind and health. The soul is not an invisible, intangible, imaginary entity. It is the very core of our personality, imagination and sensitivity. Losing our soul is not something which happens after death. It can happen now. Heaven and hell are with us now.

Beyond the Holy Loch I came to Loch Eck and after four hours walking I climbed the steep wood to the east of the loch and camped high on the hill. I walked 192 kilometres that week, mostly cross-country, over the hills, through the oak forests, along the loch sides. If I were offered a week's walking anywhere in the world, I would choose the western Highlands, but then I am naturally prejudiced!

After the first half day's walking, my heels were very sore. I changed from boots to sandals, had immediate relief from heel pain but developed much more painful blisters on the soles of my feet. I never tried sandals again. I thought the woollen socks I was wearing might be causing the blistering, so I changed to cotton, but they were worse. By avoiding hard surfaces wherever possible, and through frequent bathing in salt water, I kept the pain within tolerable limits, but realized that I still had a long way to go before I could walk 32 kilometres a day along hard surfaces with a 17–kilo weight on my back. I learned, too, that cross-country walking with this weight, while gentler on the feet and shorter in distance, took much more time and energy than most road routes. I would have to revise my routes through France and Italy.

In packing the rucksack I learned, through error, some elementary lessons about weight distribution and how to pack in such a way that what I needed during the day was easily available at the top of the sack and in the side pouches. I also discovered how to adjust the straps and belt of the rucksack so that most of the weight was resting on my hip bones. I learned to appreciate the value of plastic bags for keeping dirty clothing separate from clean.

Before this walk I had only once walked for a week and that was twenty years earlier when a group of us went from Oxford to Glastonbury. I had forgotten the experience and was now surprised at the hunger and thirst I could feel. As I became fitter the thirst lessened but my hunger for food lasted for two weeks after the walk. On the other hand, I needed less sleep, would go to bed about 11 p. m. and be wide awake by 5 a. m. or earlier.

I tried to pray when I was walking and recover the island prayer but my mind was not still. I would begin to pray, especially for the first hour's walking, but soon my mind was jumping like a grasshopper, ending in day-dreams. At other times I made no attempt to pray or think. I just looked at the oak forests, the wild flowers by the roadside, the waves on the lochs, the blue hills, and I found myself praying with the psalmist, 'All you mountains of the Lord, praise the Lord.' I was no longer trying to pray: it was as though the mountains and lochs, the forests and streams were praying for me. I felt at one with them, a feeling that was to grow on me along the road to Rome.

I finished the highland walk at Lochailort at the end of May. In the following weeks whenever I could I walked in my Berghaus boots; fast walking, always on roads, sometimes at night, sometimes in the early morning.

The night before I left Glasgow for London to begin the walk my brother and his wife put on a magnificent farewell dinner, inviting a few relatives and friends. I had the rucksack ready packed for the morning and had reduced its weight from 17 to 15.5 kilos by leaving out binoculars, a transistor and part of the cooking equipment. I wanted to reduce the weight another 2 kilos but it is all a question of balancing costs and discomforts. To travel without a tent and sleeping bag could have reduced the weight by 3.5 kilos but it would have changed the character of the walk. One of the great joys of it was the sense of freedom I could experience. With the tent and sleeping bag I could stop at any stretch of reasonably level ground and have a night's sleep. Without them I would have had the problem and expense of searching for accommodation every night and would have had to plan the route with much greater care each day. The little gas cooker, two small pots, coffee and sugar containers and an emergency supply of food weighed very little.

I left Glasgow on June 18, wondered at the emptiness of the train in which I was sitting, until I discovered I was in the wrong one. Perhaps it was as well that I was walking to Rome. That night I stayed in Weybridge with friends, Mr and Mrs Anderson. I left a spare copy of my itinerary with Mrs Anderson. 'Why leave it here?' she asked; 'is it in case you forget where you're going?' A few weeks later, when I had lost my own itinerary, I wrote to them, 'I'm now at Vézelay. Where should I be?' Two weeks after that I collected the itinerary which Mrs Anderson had forwarded to Grenoble.

Next morning, June 19, I said Mass at 7.30 in St Charles' Church, Weybridge, with the Andersons and some other friends, the O'Neills. Bob O'Neill, a school contemporary, is now a grandfather, a fact I found it hard to believe on the morning of my first day's walking but could easily accept in the evening. At Mass I prayed for my own and every other traveller's protection from Fiat, Renault and Peugeot, and for all my relatives and friends. I wanted the walk to be a continuation of this Mass, a gesture of giving to the Father, through Christ, walking towards him in search of a way across the 'cliffs of fall'. After the Mass we took some photographs, I said goodbye and started on the road to Rome.

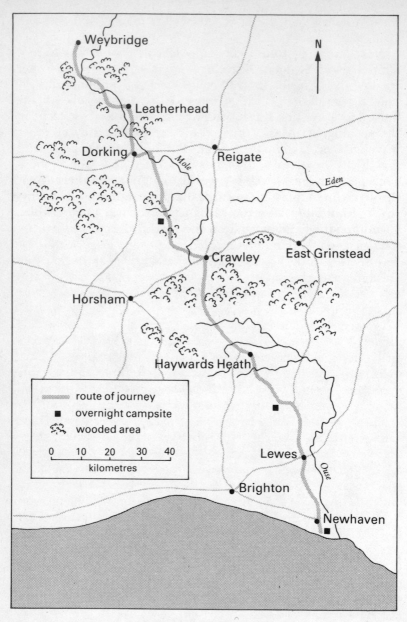

Weybridge to Newhaven

46

4

The Road to Paris

In the twelfth century there lived a monk known as Aymeric
Picaud who wrote an account of his pilgrimage through
France and Spain to the shrine of St James at Compostella.
From his story it appears he was a highly-prejudiced, rather
cross-grained pilgrim. He decided to arrange his material by
devoting separate chapters to the towns and villages he passed
through, the rivers he crossed, the people he met. Most
received negative and unsympathetic reports, especially those
outside France.

I experienced similar difficulty in arranging the material I
gathered on the road to Rome. I kept a diary in which I
jotted down a brief account of each day, including thoughts,
reflections, moods. When walking, thoughts, moods and
reflections do not come to order. They happen, like dreams.
As in dreams, they are fragmented, incoherent, apparently
inconsequential, like hearing the isolated notes of different
instruments in an orchestra. Sometimes all the varied, fragmented experiences and thoughts would come together and
for a few moments I experienced a sense of at-oneness, of
peace and great happiness. In those moments I wanted to
have all my friends, relatives and acquaintances around me
to share the moment with them, to let them know how good
God is. I write about it because I want to keep the memory
alive in myself, for I know nothing more precious. But I hope
that what I write can help other weary pilgrims, especially
disillusioned Christians, to keep plodding on until we realise
that God is nearer to us than we are to ourselves and that
the News really is Good.

I almost ended the pilgrimage within a few hundred yards

of my starting point. After a few steps along the Weybridge road I felt pain in the inside cartilage of my right knee.

Twenty-seven years earlier I had the outside cartilage removed. Six months after the operation I was still hobbling and the surgeon recommended removal of the inside cartilage as well. I visited an osteopath who poked at the knee, pulled it, twisted it, advised against the operation and recommended massage. A few months later I could run again and, apart from occasional twinges, I had no more trouble. In all the rough walking over Scottish moors and hillsides I never had any problems with muscles or joints. Now after a few steps along my pilgrim way I was walking with slightly bent knee, terrified that any sudden movement would cause the knee to lock and end the pilgrimage ingloriously. In my highland walk I had worked out a 100–degree pain scale and reckoned that my feet at their most painful were never more than 60 degrees, leaving another 40 degrees for more, bigger, septic blisters leading to complete immobility. The knee, at this stage, only merited 20 degrees, so I attributed the pain to psychosomatic anticipation and limped on.

The traffic was heavy, the sky grey. The pilgrim should start out trusting in God, full of hope and joy. My heart was in my boots, rising occasionally to the knee and then dropping back again. I hobbled on past the houses of the wealthy, set in spacious gardens. Here and there children were playing, calling to each other in well modulated tones. 'Chawles, it's Penelope's turn to ride the pony.' I thought of Glasgow's slums and the very different cries of the children. 'Hey, Jummie, gie us ra baw or ah'll bash ye,' and my mind floated off on its socialist paths, which led me very quickly into the jungle of my own ignorance.

It is not easy to pursue a coherent line of thought when walking. Walking is for contemplation not meditation, for letting thoughts lead us rather than dragging them along our ready-made paths. I did not get very far with the glorious New Society and my mind began hopping again – knee, heels, traffic, why on earth did I ever start this walk? Am I afflicted with some fatal flaw so that I never quite grasp things as they are and so am doomed to have convincing dreams and spend my life suffering the consequences of their impracticability? I knew that if I continued on this line of thought I would probably slide into a depression, so I tried to stop thinking and looked at the gardens again, the flowers, the trees. Why spoil the beauty of them with thoughts of Glasgow's slums and my own defects? I was not going to remedy Glasgow's slums or my own self-doubt by refusing to admire these lovely homes and gardens at this moment.

Whatever form the New Society may take, it must not destroy our ability to appreciate what is beautiful. There is something very wrong in such dedication to the ideals of social justice that we can no longer enjoy beautiful things for their own sake. All ideologies and 'isms', all visions and dreams, all plans and policies are dangerous and destructive if they are not conceived in hearts which are sensitive to beauty and can appreciate things for their own sake. That is why a religion which cannot see beyond rules and regulations, doctrinal and moral formulae, can have such a negative effect upon its followers. We need theologians who cultivate mysticism, and lawyers, city planners and politicians who discover and express in their work the poet and the artist in themselves. The New Society, if it is not to be more hideous than the old, needs spiritual more than economic growth, education in contemplation rather than schooling in manipulation of the world's resources and of each other.

Having got lost in the region of Leatherhead, I was so impatient with myself that I walked past The Pilgrims' Rest, a delightful looking fourteenth-century pub in the town, because it was twenty minutes until opening time and I did not want to be late arriving in Rome. The pub was built to cater for the needs of the Canterbury pilgrims in the days when men went on holiday not to the sea, lakes or mountains, but to visit the relics of some saint. They believed that the relics contained a kind of heavenly radiation which could be passed on to all who venerated them, guiding them safely to the same heavenly destination. There was a brisk trade in relics, and towns and cities were rated according to the value of the relics they possessed and the cures the relics could effect. This led to many a sudden discovery of valuable relics in the most unlikely places and multiplication of miracle stories confirming that the relics were genuine. Trade followed the revelations.

But there were many other reasons for going on pilgrimage besides relic hunting. Penitents were sometimes sent on pilgrimage as a penance for their sins, others might go voluntarily, some shod, some barefoot, some walking all the way, some travelling by horse or mule, in groups or alone. There were also those who went on pilgrimage because they had stout legs, liked travelling and wanted a bit of adventure; forerunners of today's hitch-hikers. Sometimes criminals who were too well known in their own neighbourhood joined pilgrim groups, robbed them and then ran away until they needed more money and found another pilgrim group. There were hundreds of pilgrimage centres throughout Europe. The most famous, apart from Canterbury, were St James of Compostella (Santiago), St Peter's in Rome, and Jerusalem.

I do not think that all these reasons account for the popularity of pilgrimages in the Middle Ages. Walking on foot to some 'holy' place answers a deep religious need. The Greeks went to Delphi, Muslims go to Mecca, some English people go to Stonehenge. It is a symbolic gesture, a search for our real destination, a kind of sacramental journey, a sign that we are in search of an answer to our deepest longings, and the journey is undertaken in the belief that there is an answer. R.L. Stevenson wrote, 'To travel hopefully is a better thing than to arrive.' On the road the pilgrim learns that searching for God is already to have found him and that direction is much more important than destination, because God is not just an end, nor a beginning, but for us he is always a beginning without end.

They were a motley crowd those medieval pilgrims: saints and sinners, mystics and criminals, a cross-section of 'the people of God', their motives as mixed as their persons. I thought about them as I walked, and felt phoney. I was setting off, very grateful to modern technology for my frame rucksack, lightweight nylon tent, Berghaus boots, gas cooker, compass, maps, travellers' cheques and an insurance policy against theft or injury. The medieval pilgrims set off for Spain,

Rome or Jerusalem with their cloak, pouch, gourd, sandals and little else. They faced terrible hazards, far worse than Fiats, Renaults and Peugeots which can usually be avoided. They faced danger from robbers, rivers, storms, disease, hunger and wild animals.

Aymeric Picaud, in his twelfth-century guide for pilgrims to Compostella, warns his readers of what they are to expect when they come to rivers which can be crossed only by ferry. 'May the ferrymen be damned! Get in with only a few passengers because if there are too many, the boat will capsize forthwith. When they have the money the ferrymen load on so many pilgrims that the boat overturns and the pilgrims are drowned, then the boatmen evilly rejoice, having plundered the dead of their goods.' The pilgrims are not even safe on the bridges, or on some main roads, where there are toll collectors. Aymeric comments on these: 'May they go to the devil! They come out in the pilgrims' way with two or three staves to extort an unjust toll, and if anyone refuses to pay up in accordance with their demands, they strike with their sticks and seize the tax, injuring the victims . . . We demand that all these men, until they have expiated their sins by long penitence and a reduction of the taxes they demand, be placed under sentence of excommunication.'

Ferrymen and toll men were not the only unpleasant people he met. He describes the Navarrais and the Basques, whom he finds similar to, and reckons to be of the same race and character as, the Scots. Of the Navarrais he writes: 'To hear them eat you would take them for dogs and pigs; to hear them talk makes you think of barking dogs. They are a barbaric people full of pranks, dark of countenance, ugly in appearance, debauched, perverse, faithless, disloyal, corrupt, sensuous, drinkers, experts in violence, fierce and savage, dishonest and false, impious and rough, cruel and quarrelsome, immune to all feelings, inclined to every vice and iniquity.' Even when the pilgrimage was over, the danger was not. When the relics were on view at the pilgrimage centre, people could be crushed to death in the devotional rush. One of the reasons given for the official discouragement of women pilgrims was their greater liability to death by crushing when the relics were exposed!

I walked past The Pilgrims' Rest because it was not yet opening time and found my own pilgrim's rest a few minutes before closing time when I was well south of Dorking on a very minor road. One and a half pints of shandy and Mrs Anderson's sandwiches did my mood a power of good, but I was staggering badly when I began walking again an hour later, not from the shandy, but from stiffness in my legs and pain in my heels, which had now caught up with and overtaken the knee pain.

I was wearing a pair of woollen socks with cotton socks covering them. Inside the boots I had a pair of sponge insoles to give further protection, but the insoles kept working their way down the boots, gathering in a crumpled heap under the instep. I stopped and bought a tube of glue. According to the directions, the insoles should then have become an inseparable part of the boot, but after an hour's walking they had reverted to their crumpled, but now stickier, state. It took me two more days before I hit on the obvious remedy which then saved my heels from serious pain the whole way to Rome. I tore the insoles in half, placed each half carefully over the woollen socks so that they covered the base and back of each heel, held the insole in place while putting the cotton sock over the woollen. Besides protecting my heels, this simple remedy delighted my Scottish soul because one insole was now doing the work of two.

When I had covered 32 kilometres and was beginning to drag my feet, I began looking for a place to camp. In the highland walk there was never any problem about camping. My route was through wild and desolate country and I camped wherever I could find water. But Surrey is neither wild nor desolate and there is no wrath to match the wrath of an angry farmer. I approached a farm with acres of level pasture. The farmer was loading cases of eggs into a van, assisted by his daughter. 'May I camp in that field for the night?' I asked, pointing to his acres. 'It's far too risky,' said the farmer, 'unless you want your tent ripped and chewed and walked over by the cows.' 'But Daddy,' said the daughter, 'he could camp here under the oak tree and be safe from the cows.' 'I don't want anyone camping under my oak tree,' said Dad. I wished them a good evening and hobbled on, feeling very sorry for myself.

A mile further on I saw an old-fashioned bungalow bordering a large field in which two horses were grazing. The owner was a most courteous man, took me out to the field, apologized for its bumpiness and drove out the horses. He showed me a water trough and told me not to hesitate to come to the house if I needed anything. It is amazing what a few kind words can do. I no longer felt so tired and for the first time on that first day's walking I began to relish the thought of ten weeks on the road. I pitched the tent, washed myself and my socks under the tap and prepared supper; a packet soup, a tin of stew (not Irish), tinned fruit, cheese and coffee. During the highland walk and on the island I had become accustomed to eating in the open with the flies and various species of crawling things, mostly ants, for company. At first I tried to get rid of them, then I began to ignore them and finally I took to feeding them.

The moments after supper were the most peaceful of the day as I sat outside the tent with a cup of coffee and let the day play back to me in memory, relishing its good moments and reliving the feelings and thoughts that had come to me. It was not a deliberate attempt to pray, but it usually became a prayer of gratitude for God's goodness. Sleep, even on this hard ground, was not a problem. I was tired out and I had learned how to curl up on hard ground, my legs resting on the rucksack slightly above the level of my head.

I woke around 5 a.m. to a misty dawn and began the morning ritual. Still in the sleeping bag, I leaned forward, unzipped the front of the tent, groped with my left hand to find the gas cooker, which I kept along with my boots and socks in the space between the inner tent and the flysheet. I filled a small pot with water from the flask, set it on the gas cooker just outside the tent and started the day with a mug of strong black coffee, which gave me the energy to crawl out of my sleeping bag and wash.

At 6.30 a.m. I was on the road for Crawley, my socks,

sodden with dew, hanging out to dry on a line at the back of the rucksack. The knee pain had almost disappeared and my heels were no longer complaining. Feet behave like children. They demand attention, and if attention is not given, they throw tantrums and exact a terrible vengeance. During the first two weeks of the walk I used to remove boots and socks after every hour's walking, bathe my feet if possible, or at least given them air, and wash my socks every day. My heels slowly responded to this treatment and started their complaints later each day, but it was only in the last three weeks of the walk that they accepted the pounding uncomplainingly and by that time they were as hard as leather. Even at their worst, the heel pain was never more than 30 degrees.

It was cool and the roads were quiet for the first hour's walking, but the mist was rising into a cloudless sky. I reached Crawley at 9.30 a. m. in a lather of sweat, feeling as if I had done a full day's walking. One hour and much bacon and eggs later I was ready for the road again, but a few miles south of Haywards Heath I suddenly felt very weary and had my first experience of foot cramp. I tried a shandy for extra mileage but the rest only made me feel stiff as well as cramped and so I called in at a nearby house with a field adjoining. A young boy came to the door, gaped at my rucksack, then grinned. 'Mum's out, but she'll be back soon and I'm sure she won't mind.' So we sat chatting about my rucksack, tents and his school. He was completely at ease, a characteristic he must have inherited from his mother who arrived soon afterwards, showed no sign of surprise or suspicion, told me I was welcome to the field for the night and later reappeared with a cup of coffee. I have rarely appreciated a cup of coffee so much.

After supper, as I sat outside the tent, I let the day play back to me, the roads I had walked, the villages I passed through, the faces of people I had seen. It had been a good day but the high point of it was the moment this woman had given me a cup of coffee. I wondered at this reaction and began on a line of thought which remained with me throughout the walk and is still with me. Why did I experience such pleasure from that cup of coffee? It was certainly not the quality of the instant coffee. Why had I felt so sorry for myself on the first evening when the farmer would not let me camp under his oak tree?

On the road, as an anonymous human being, I became more sensitive to people's reactions, whether of acceptance or rejection. Kindness elated me: suspicion, which was frequent especially in France, or hostility, which I encountered only once, depressed me. Because I was anonymous I felt much more vulnerable and I began to realize how I am protected, quite unconsciously, by my status as a Jesuit priest. This awareness later led me to decide to keep my anonymity on the road to Rome, never to volunteer the information that I was a priest and not to use my status to obtain free board and lodging at presbyteries or religious houses on the way. Of course, it sometimes happens that if introduced as a Jesuit priest I incur more hostility than if I had remained anonymous, but this kind of hostility does not hurt as much and I don't take it as personal.

These reflections led me on to the whole question of religious poverty. People laugh cynically, and with reason, when they hear about religious poverty, especially Jesuit poverty. I spent nine years of my Jesuit life living in an historical monument, which included a museum containing many priceless art treasures, mostly gifts, ancient chalices, monstrances heavy with jewels, Rembrandts, Dürers and other works of art. Inside this magnificent building lived a community of Jesuits, many of whom practised a severe personal poverty, wearing suits green with age and streaked with ancient dinner stains, broken shoes, holes in the heels of their socks. Their rooms were sparsely furnished, uncomfortable and drafty. My own room at one period was so small that I had to fold up the bed each morning to provide room to sit at my desk. They were good men, who worked very hard, taught well and earned the respect and affection of many of their pupils. Part of me admired this asceticism, but I could never reconcile this personal practice of poverty with the grandeur of the building and the wealth of its possessions. This poverty was somehow too secret, too private, too exclusive and it was not immediately clear who was benefiting from it. I tried to practise this poverty, but for me it became negative, a nagging, niggling poverty of prohibitions – 'you should not have this and you should not have that'. I was neither able to abandon myself to this form of poverty nor able to enjoy what I failed to renounce.

During my years in Glasgow I began to understand poverty differently. My life there was much less sheltered, less secure, and more exposed to questioning. I became much more aware of my own spiritual helplessness and often the only prayer I could make with sincerity was, 'Lord, save me or I'll perish.' My previous certainties seemed to be collapsing around me. Circumstances reduced me to this state, not any virtue of mine. I was only conscious of my inadequacy and weakness. Yet it was in this state that I began to experience the power of faith and to have a new understanding of Christ's words, 'Blessed are the poor in spirit'. Being poor in that sense means knowing our own helplessness and putting our trust in God. There are no situations where he is not present. He is in the darkness as well as in the light, in failure as well as in health, in the crucifixion as well as in the resurrection. It was as though God were asking, 'Do you really trust me?' Yes, Lord, but help my distrust.' Then he would answer, 'Then don't be afraid to go out and meet the people around you. Don't be afraid to listen to them, to acknowledge the truth of what they say, even if it conflicts with your own beliefs and you do not know how to reconcile the two. Don't be afraid of honesty, even if it deprives you of certainty and you no longer know what you are.'

I began to see poverty as a way to freedom, a letting go of all those securities which make me feel safe but which are, in fact, barriers to true freedom. The greatest barrier is a conviction of our own rightness and righteousness. As the truth dawned on me, I became less afraid of questions and challenges, less anxious to 'help' people and more content to be with them. It was like learning to swim. I began to learn that I could float when out of my depth. I now thought of poverty as a kind of swimming exercise, a practice which enables us to let go of the rail of our own security and certainty so that we can learn to float in God.

Now I could see more clearly why I had found the practice of poverty so negative and niggling. For me it was like substituting the smooth bath rail for a piece of barbed wire stretched along the shallow end. It was not only painful to grasp, but it also kept me from floating and trusting. A Religious vowed to poverty can be as attached to his piece of barbed wire as the tycoon to his bar of gold. A religious vow of poverty is a means to an end. The means is the letting go of certain forms of security – wealth, status and family ties in order to become a freer instrument of God's love and peace. But to take a vow of poverty and then be preoccupied with the details of material poverty in a nagging, petty way is to defeat the purpose of the vow. Similarly, a preoccupation with one's own 'religious perfection', being afraid to let other people speak their minds in case they argue too convincingly against the truths of faith; all these attitudes run counter to the openness, availability and vulnerability which the vow of poverty is meant to engender.

During the walk, my greater sensitivity to people's kindness or indifference helped me to recognize my own unconscious need for security, besides the very conscious clinging to the security provided by my rucksack. I only felt able to swim in the very calm waters of poverty and was not ready for the rough seas of real penury. So I kept my rucksack with its traveller's cheques and insurance, assuring myself that all ideas are dangerous if we are not humble before them and acknowledge our own inability to attain them.

As I sat drinking that cup of coffee I started thinking about the meaning of the religious vow of poverty. The normal meaning of poverty is deprivation which is a social evil. What connection is there between the two? The tragedy is that we have to ask the question. Religious can be found practising a rigorous religious poverty within expensive establishments set in areas of social deprivation. The two forms of poverty are sometimes literally separated by a high wall. Poverty, in the sense of material, social, intellectual, spiritual deprivation is an evil, not a virtue, to be rejected, not accepted. It is blasphemous to think that God, who gives himself to us in Christ so that men may have life and have it more abundantly, wants people to accept deprivation. *Gloria Dei vivens homo*, wrote St Irenaeus: The Glory of God is man alive. If we really believe this, then Christian worship and service of God must include working with all our strength to eliminate poverty. 'I was thirsty and you gave me to drink. I was hungry and you gave me to eat.' As far as men and women vowed to poverty are concerned, it is not enough for us to feed beggars at the back door. If we are serious, we must be with the poor in their poverty, know it, share it, feel the pain, indignity and injustice of it, pray in our helplessness and in the strength that comes from this abandonment. Through this practice of poverty we can use the gifts God has given us to change the structures of our society which perpetuate this deprivation.

During the cup of coffee I had only started on these thoughts about poverty. I was very tired and soon fell asleep, looking forward to tomorrow when I had only about 19 kilometres more to walk to Newhaven and then no more walking until I arrived in France on Sunday afternoon.

I was on the road by 6.30 a. m.: a bright, clear day with a cool breeze and excellent views across the South Downs. It was on this road that I had my first encounter with the police, who pulled in ahead of me and asked me where I was going. 'Newhaven,' I told them. They wished me good luck and drove on without any further questioning. The French police were to be more thorough. I had not yet made a decision about avoiding presbyteries and religious houses and had phoned up the parish priest at Newhaven asking if I could stay for the night. He explained that he had just moved into the house and that I was welcome if I did not mind chaos and looking after myself. I assured him that I was well accustomed to both and arrived at 1.30 p. m. The house *was* in chaos, but to have a roof over my head, a bed and running water was luxury. That evening we went into Brighton for supper. It was good to share a meal again and we put the Church to right in the course of it. When we returned to Newhaven at 10 p. m. I felt no tiredness and sat up late finishing the first instalment of a series of articles which I

58

had promised to send during the walk to *The Tablet*, a Catholic weekly.

Next morning being a Sunday I said one of the parish Masses in Newhaven and caught the 11.30 ferry for Dieppe, grateful for this stretch of the way where I could sit in comfort, cover distance and yet take, in Belloc's words, 'no wheeled thing'. At this stage I was not at all resolute about avoiding lifts. I wanted to enjoy the walk and if my feet became too painful, or the walking too exhausting, I was certainly going to take lifts. As I sat on deck examining the second of my fourteen sections of map, a passport officer approached, introduced himself and asked me where I was going. During the war, he told me, he had been trained as a commando to walk 80 kilometres a day carrying a 41-kilo pack. He had been taken prisoner, escaped from a POW camp in northern Italy, and walked his way across the Alps and the south of France, begging, stealing and sleeping out in the open. 'Amazing what you can do when you have to,' he said, 'but I would advise you not to try more than 48 kilometres a day.' My plan to walk 32 kilometres a day with a 16-kilo pack seemed like a senior citizen's outing and the thought of the heroic deeds of men of old did nothing for my confidence.

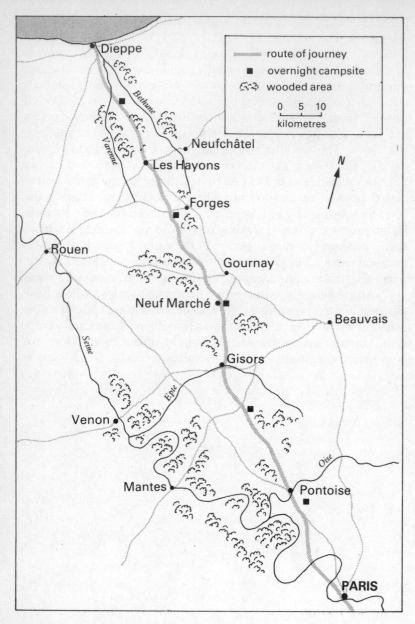

Dieppe to Paris

5

The Continent

We landed at Dieppe at 3.30 p. m. I hurried past the open market by the harbour with its strong smell of shellfish and the occasional whiff of Gauloise. On the boat I had studied the evening's route and was searching for the D. 154, a minor road, because I wanted to avoid the main N. 15 to Paris. I carried the map in my hand with the compass tied to my wrist, but for all my attempts at navigation, I ended up on the N. 15, an open, uninteresting road. However, the traffic was light and the road straight and I had covered 20 kilometres before I began to tire. About twenty-five years ago I spent a summer in France and was reasonably fluent in French, but my vocabulary, grammar and syntax were buried deep in memory and beyond immediate recall. I tried to call up phrases for my first camping attempt. *Je veux camper*, sounded a bit abrupt, but it would have to do. It did not do. The old man whom I first approached, said, '*Pardon monsieur*', so I tried again. He understood this time, threw up his hands, the shoulders following, pouted his lips and gave me a stream of French which included '*gendarmerie*' and '*défendu*', so I wished him good evening and walked on.

The sky had become overcast and I felt the first drops of rain. Were all French farmers like this one? Was that why Ian Tweedie had recommended cemeteries for the night? I preferred the wrath of the living and tried again, but with a much more subtle approach. The farm was set in acres of lush grass. I removed the water flask from my rucksack, rang the front door bell and tried to look helpless. 'Excuse me,' I said to the man who answered, 'I don't speak French very well. I am a Scot walking to Paris, and I wonder if you could give me some drinking water.' 'Certainly', he replied and returned with the flask. 'I was wondering if you could recommend a place where I could camp for the night.' He led me to the end of the garden, pointed to a field and said, 'It's yours,' so I pitched my tent in the drizzle and drank some onion soup.

'It's yours,' he had said. That was another joy of camping. Wherever I camped, it was my place for the night and I enjoyed possession while I had it; but it was a free possession, free in the sense that I was not bound or tied to it in any way. I had a kind of detached attachment to it which is, presumably, what Ignatius means by 'indifference'. The stoic makes himself indifferent and detached, so that he is neither crushed by sorrow in misfortune, nor elated by joy in good fortune; whereas in Christian asceticism detachment is for a new kind of attachment, for joy in creation unspoiled by possessiveness either of the creature or of oneself, because one has found God in all creatures and all creatures in him. I could have pursued this line of thought if I had been detached enough but there were kennels at the bottom of the garden and the dogs, disturbed by my presence, were barking neurotically and stopped only when I crawled into the tent, closed it up and lay still.

On Monday morning I was up before six and wandered around the lovely old farm buildings which included rabbit hutches housing large white rabbits with sad pink eyes. I used to enjoy pottering about in the early morning, postponing the moment when I had to put on the rucksack again and start the day's walking. It was cold and cloudy when I set off, still on the main N.15 until I reached Les Grandes Ventes, where I called in at the church for Mass at 8.00 a. m. The Mass was celebrated at a side altar by an elderly priest and a congregation of six elderly women, all dressed in black. Congregation and celebrant seemed to be in a world of their own private devotions and I felt like an intruder.

When I started on the road again I was feeling annoyed and then grew angry at my own annoyance. I began to argue with myself. 'For heaven's sake stop moaning and complaining. Why can't you just be glad that Mass is being celebrated and that these elderly women who look so beaten by life can find help in its celebration? Have you no sense of wonder in you? Are you so preoccupied with outward appearances that you can't appreciate the marvel that is happening whenever and however Mass is celebrated? The almighty and eternal God speaks in this Mass and tells us who he is: "Take and eat, this is my body given for you." ' Having listened to this lecture from one part of myself, the other part argued back. 'It is because I can marvel at what is happening that I complain about the manner of it. It is not this priest and this congregation I am complaining about. I felt like an intruder at this Mass and yet the Mass celebrates Christ's love for all men.'

I was complaining about a whole attitude and pattern of behaviour in the Catholic Church, an attitude which turns the Mass into a private devotion for the chosen few and when I meet it, I feel robbed. Christ came for all men, for the outcast and sinner, the stranger and alien. He welcomed them, he gave them a vision of their worth and of their dignity; 'Bring in the lame, the halt and the blind.' But we have encased the whole wonderful message in a package of rules and regulations, prohibitions and warnings so that it is no longer recognizable to most, and Christ can no longer speak to the majority of men.

I grumbled my way through the drizzle and when it turned to rain I called in at a café and had two diminutive cups of coffee, which were very expensive and made me grateful for the gas stove and pots I had brought with me. Light rain continued all morning and I kept walking until I found a *restaurant des routiers* (a transport café) at Les Hayons, where they were serving lunch for 12 francs. The lorry drivers, enormous swarthy men, were sitting around tables littered with bottles and carafes of wine. Whenever a new driver entered, he went round the tables and shook hands with all the others before sitting down to eat. The meal was enormous. An excellent hors-d'oeuvres with the unpromising name *crudités* which was a lettuce and tomato salad, followed by steak and chips, a vast cheeseboard, ice cream and a carafe of wine. I had walked 24 kilometres on a piece of bread for breakfast and did justice to every course of the meal. When I began walking again I felt very sleepy. I often fall asleep sitting, I have even fallen asleep when talking, waking up to hear myself finishing a sentence. I have fallen asleep standing, but I had never come so near to falling asleep when walking as on this occasion. It was still raining, but I went into a field and slept under a tree for half an hour and then walked, footsore but not tired, until 6 p. m. when I tried a farm house for camping. A studious-looking girl answered the door and, when I had explained myself, she said she would have to see *maman* who was milking the cows. *Maman* told us that we would have to ask *papa* who was mending a fence. *Papa* readily agreed, apologized for the state of his field, which was muddy and covered with cow flop which the tractor had spread evenly all around. I was now so tired that I did not mind the mess or the drizzle, thanked God for the dry clothing and dry tent and slept soundly until a cock crowed in my ear at 4 a. m., a call to prayer and to greet the dawn; but I turned over and slept for another three hours.

I was on the road again at 8.30 a. m., along the route I had planned, which avoided the main roads. I had seen this countryside many times in pictures and films of the two world wars: long straight roads with tall trees on both sides, a flat or gently undulating countryside. As I walked past the vast wheat and maize fields, apple orchards and old farms with their beautiful Normandy cattle, it was hard to believe that this had been an area of human slaughter.

I reached Argueil an hour later, a small village with a quaint baroque church whose benches had little doors on them. I wondered about the little doors. Were they to keep undesirable neighbours from praying in the same bench as yourself? In the village I bought breakfast, a loaf of bread, tomatoes, bananas, camembert cheese and a litre of milk. I usually had breakfast after two or three hours walking and afterwards I read the office of readings and morning prayer from the Roman breviary. Sometimes a phrase from one of the psalms or prayers would strike me and keep returning to my mind during the day, but it had to be something very simple. Its slow, rhythmic repetition in time with my steps

64

would still my mind. This rhythmic form of prayer helped me to understand why I had always found the rosary and litanies, traditional Catholic forms of prayer, so impossibly difficult. I am sure they began as pilgrim prayers and should be said walking. I am told that there are roads in Spain where the distances between places are measured by the number of rosaries you can say.

The rosary is centuries old. It is a simple way of recalling the gospels, the incarnation, passion and resurrection of Christ. Each of these three mysteries is divided into five decades, each decade consisting of one Our Father, ten Hail Marys and a Glory be to the Father. During each decade a different aspect of the mystery is considered. The mystery of the incarnation, for example, called the Joyful Mysteries, is divided into the angel's annunciation to Mary, Mary's visit to her cousin Elizabeth, the birth of Christ, his presentation in the temple after his birth, and the finding of the child in the temple at Jerusalem. In my own home we used to say five decades of the rosary every night before going to bed. I disliked the practice as a child and used to try to speed up the prayers to have them over and done with, or hope my mother would forget about them, which she never did. On some evenings she would say she wanted to stay on and pray and we left her there and went to another room. I used to wonder why she wanted to go on praying and felt uneasy at my own boredom. I never overcame the boredom and eventually abandoned the rosary. It was while walking to Rome that I came to appreciate it. It is a rhythmic prayer and I could vary the rhythm, sometimes a few syllables to each step, sometimes a few steps to one syllable. I could pray almost effortlessly for an hour in this way, whereas if I were to try and spend an hour praying the rosary while sitting still, I should be exhausted at the end of it.

Sometimes I sang prayers as I walked and the Caribbean version of the Our Father would bring back memories of crowded Masses at Turnbull Hall. I could see the familiar faces again and start on a kind of litany in which I saw each one of the congregation and asked God to be with them, to smile on them and make them express his goodness. At other times I did what I had learned to do on the island and on the highland walk. I just looked at the fields and the orchards, at the farm buildings, the trees and the gestures of their branches. My mind would become still, empty of thought and the beat of my feet would say to me, *Qu'il est bon, qu'il est bon, qu'il est bon le bon Dieu!*

After a large breakfast and long rest outside Argueil, I kept walking until 4.30 p. m. when I reached a village called Neuf Marché, where I stopped to buy food for supper. It was only when I stopped that I realized how tired I was and the rucksack felt like lead. Outside the village I saw a house bordering a field and entered the garden gate. On the balcony of the house a huge alsatian was growling and as I approached it leaped on its chain and barked. A young woman appeared round the corner of the balcony. 'What do you want?', she snapped, as close a human imitation of an alsatian as I have seen. I explained that I had been walking all day, was looking for a place to camp for the night and asked if she could please tell me to whom the field belonged. 'Get away from here!' was her reply. Just as the friendliness of the farmer's family the night before had cheered me, so this woman enraged me. I asked if she could speak English, as my French could not do justice to the comments forming in my mind about this land of *liberté, egalité et fraternité.* 'Certainly not,' she replied and took off round the corner leaving myself and the chained and howling alsatian full of impotent fury.

I limped off, my anger exacerbated by the pain in my heels and whole body, until I found a river where I camped, well out of sight of the main road. It was a mild, dry evening and after I had set up the tent, washed and eaten by the side of the river, I began to wonder at my sudden rage. I could now better understand Aymeric Picaud's descriptions of the Navarrais. He probably met them when he was very tired, hungry and suffering from blisters. My anger was so pointless. It did nothing for the lady and was just as ineffective as the chained alsatian's. I suddenly felt very sorry, not so much at this particular incident, but for all the harsh words I had ever spoken and all the hurt I had caused, especially to friends. We do not have each other for long.

Next morning it was still mild and dry. I lingered by the riverside, reluctant to start because my heels were still tender. When I did eventually get started I was back again on the main road, which had a broad grass verge. I walked on this verge, an uneven surface, broken every few steps by drainage ditches, which slowed down my pace but saved my heels. At midday I found another *restaurant des routiers*. As I had cut all my maps in order to save weight, I found myself without the Michelin key for deciphering some of the markings on my current map from Dieppe to Paris. I asked one of the *routiers* if he could help. Within a minute there were six of them, all volunteering information and some of them offered me a lift to Paris. We parted with solemn handshakes and wishes for *bon courage*.

That night I camped on a farm track with cabbages on one side and maize on the other. The next day was Thursday, June 26, and I had completed the first week's walking. I was on the road at 7.30 a. m. and after an hour's walking the rucksack still felt light and my heels were painless. Outside the village of Chars I caught up with a group of children on their way to school. 'What have you in there?' they asked, pointing to my rucksack. 'My house, my kitchen, bed, wardrobe and books,' I said. 'Where are you going?' 'To Rome. Would you like to come?' 'Yes,' said the smallest, who was dragging his feet to school.

There was a rhythm to my walking now and I was much less tired at the end of the day. My mind, too, was becoming more still. In walking it is as though ideas in the head are shaken up and some start travelling downwards, to the heart where they become a full-blooded knowing, which sets up a physical reaction. Today the word 'grace' travelled downwards. 'God's grace is a gratuitous gift. We do not merit it, earn it, deserve it. It is freely given.' I had known this in my head since childhood. I even knew that there were different kinds of grace and had learned the distinctions. In theology I was introduced to further distinctions and theories as to how 'it' works but it was all very cerebral, abstract and boring.

As I walked, the truth that God first loved us, and not for

any merit of our own, broke in on me and I wanted to laugh and cry at the same time in the wonder of it. I prayed, 'Glory to you, O God, always greater. Touch me with your presence. I want nothing else. Cleanse my mind and heart of its false images of you and put a new heart into me which can know you in loving you.'

I hesitate to write these experiences in case they make me out to be a better person than I am, in case the writing is a subtle form of vanity and conceit. But I write them because I know that grace is gratuitous, not something I have earned or deserve, and because I know that the goodness of God is far more important and powerful than my inhibitions. Faith is so simple but we make it so complicated. But the God to whom we turn is the God who is already close to us, who takes us as we are, warts and all.

That afternoon I reached Pontoise and called in at a bank to change travellers' cheques. It was a very prosperous looking bank, all glass, chrome and polish, with a row of neat typists busy at their typewriters and calculators. When I entered its hygienic cleanliness I suddenly realized how dirty and grubby I was. I took off my pack, rested it against the counter and rummaged for my jacket which held my travellers' cheques and passport. There was a vile smell of camembert, oozing now after a day's maturing in the warmth of my sun-drenched rucksack. Sensitive nostrils twitched. I was served quickly and vowed never to carry camembert again.

Pontoise was heavy with traffic and I walked quickly, hoping to get clear of the town before finding a camping place for the night. At one point I attempted a short cut across a maze of roads and ended up on a mound of high ground separating two motorways, which then converged. I waited for a break in the stream of traffic, the object of much hooting and gesticulating by law-loving French motorists. There is no one more censorious, more full of self-righteous indignation than the motorist who spots a pedestrian breaking the highway code. Their indignation is in direct proportion to the price of their car and the helplessness of the pedestrian. My hatred of motorists was only just beginning, a quiet smould-

ering, which spread and was fanned into irrational rage by
the time I reached Rome.

I walked for another two hours after the motorway,
penetrating deeper into suburban jungle, and came to rest in
a potato patch clearing next to a garage. An obliging garage
receptionist told me that the owners of the patch were on
holiday and would not be home for another ten days. I
recommend potato patch camping provided there is no wind.
The tent was not too steady and sagged badly on the soft
ground, but the furrows were comfortable to lie on and the
tent did not collapse until I had crawled out of it in the
morning to breakfast by the nettle border.

The potato patch was only 15 kilometres from the centre
of Paris. I intended entering the city by Montmartre, so that
I could visit the chapel in which St Ignatius and his first
Jesuit companions had taken their first vows in 1534 when
they were still university students. I was going to stay in Paris
over the weekend. I would not wish the walk into Paris on
my worst enemy. I had no map of the city and walked by
compass, eventually getting a bearing on the Eiffel Tower,
but I could not keep on course. The roadway planners of
modern cities cater only for wheeled things and their only
acknowledgement of the pedestrian is in notices forbidding
him to proceed. I walked on resolutely, climbed fences if they
were low enough, cursed the many impenetrable cul-de-sacs,
and eventually found myself well to the west of Montmartre.

I bought a street map of Paris, and at 4 p. m. reached the
rue de Grenelle, where I had stayed in the Jesuit house for a
few days in 1949. The French Jesuits welcomed me and
showed no great surprise that I had come on foot. *Les Anglais*
are usually eccentric and must never be expected to behave
normally. The house is cosmopolitan and I met American,
Asian, Indian and African Jesuits on that first evening. You
have to live for a while in discomfort in the open to appreciate
the luxury of a roof, a bed, running water, meals at a table;
and you have to experience solitude to appreciate company.
I did not feel tired, and I chatted for hours besides washing all
my clothes and writing cards and my diary. On the Saturday
morning I felt so rested that I decided to start walking again

that afternoon instead of staying in Paris until Monday. I spent the morning writing and had two hours in the library with volumes of Larousse, looking up articles on Pilgrims and Pilgrimage, Vézelay, Taizé, Cluny, Grenoble.

At 3 p. m. I left the Jesuit house and sauntered along the Seine, stopping at the secondhand bookstalls on my way to Notre Dame. The square in front of the cathedral was crowded with tourists, mostly young ones. Within the cathedral there were hundreds more sightseers, but their chatter and movement cannot disturb the solemn stillness of the place. I entered to pray, but I could not at first, at least not the 'Lord, save me from blisters, sunstroke and motorists' type of prayer. I sat and let the vastness of the cathedral and the lines of its arches engender an inner silence and do the praying for me, the kind of prayer I had experienced on the island, not so much an activity I engaged in as something which engaged me when I was still. I sat thanking God. The builders of Notre Dame had translated this attitude into stone. Following the lines of its pillars to its arches lifts the heart up to pray. Then I had a distraction as I looked at those arches. I remembered the story of an archbishop, who preached once in his Gothic cathedral on the theme 'Authority in the Church'. He illustrated his topic not with reference to Scripture, but to the cathedral's architecture. He explained that as the arch is to the cathedral, so is the archbishop to his local Church. He then described the function of the arch: 'a heavy body, imposed upon the rest of the edifice, holding it in a state of strained immobility'.

I left the cathedral, stood for a moment blinded by the bright sunlight of the square and then started on my way along the Seine. It was a depressing stretch of road, hot and dusty, with warehouses and factories. The euphoric mood of prayerful praise in Notre Dame was giving way before a massive attack of minor irritations. I was hot, sticky, grimy, thirsty and the sun was hurting my eyes. Leaving Paris was as difficult as entering for the pedestrian. I scuttled my way across ring roads by compass, hoping to find the main N.5 and be well clear of suburbia by nightfall. My mood had changed from 'Glory to God' to 'Blast them all, especially

makers of ring roads and all who drive on them'. There was
a stage in my life when I would have tried to fight down these
feelings and force myself to pray. Now I just show God my
irritation as if to remind him that he has still a lot of work
to do, and then the irritability begins to dissolve.

At 6 p. m. I was still in the Paris of factories and warehouses. I stopped at a café for a beer and asked the barman
if there were any shops nearby where I could buy a canister
of gas. An elderly man in the corner of the bar offered to take
me to a shop when I had finished my beer. He introduced
himself as 'Bernard'. He had fought with the Free French in
the last war and had been stationed at Winchester, a city
second only to Paris in his estimation. When I had finished
my beer we started out for the shops. Bernard had a severe
limp. I assured him that there was no need for him to come
with me and that if he could give me directions, I could easily
find my way. He would not hear of it. He loved *rendre service*
he told me, especially to *les Anglais* who lived in such beautiful
cities as Winchester. He suggested that we first call at his
house where I could leave my rucksack. His house was a
room and kitchen, cluttered with bits and pieces but warm
and friendly, like its occupant. We set out for the shops a
kilometre away.

Bernard proceeded very slowly, partly because of his limp,
but also because he did not want me to miss anything of the
history, geography, life and times of the inhabitants. He
seemed to know everyone who passed and would stop to
introduce me as *un Anglais*. When I told him that I was *un
Ecossais* he said he knew that, but in France we always say
Anglais. We reached the shops. Bernard could not remember
where the gas shop was and started to make inquiries. Each
inquiry was preceded by a potted autobiography leading into
his introduction of *l'Anglais* and his needs. When we eventually found the shop I tried to hurry the proceedings and avoid
interminable explanations from Bernard. I began to ask for
a canister of gas, but Bernard was not to be deprived of the
love of his life, *rendre service*, and he cut in on me. *Madame*
behind the counter looked like a retired infant teacher. 'If
you will speak one at a time, perhaps I shall be able to serve

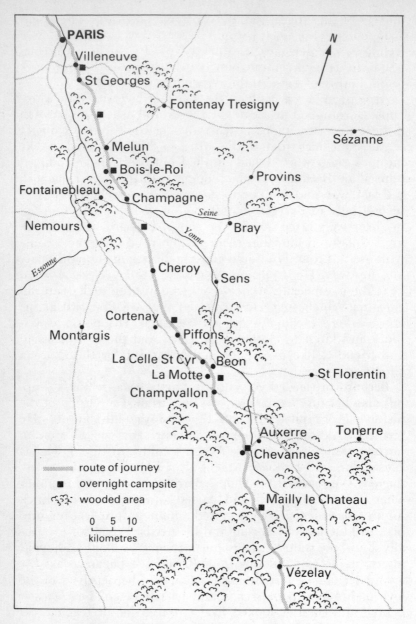

Paris to Vézelay

you,' she said. Bernard, like the ancient Nestor, began to speak. 'I am Bernard, and this is my friend, *un Anglais*.' He then went on to his wartime experiences, the beauties of Winchester and his delight in rendering service. *Madame's* growing impatience was quite lost on him.

It was 8 p. m. when we finally parted. If I reach old age, I hope I can be as full of life and warmth as Bernard. An hour and a half later I decided to shelter for the night on a building site. As I ate my supper on the damp, concrete floor two black rats scurried past. However much I tried to think of them as fellow creatures, I could not persuade myself to stay the night there and moved to tractor-churned ground a few hundred metres away. Not surprisingly, I had a broken night's sleep.

At Villeneuve I followed the sound of bells to the church door. The parish priest introduced himself and invited me to concelebrate Mass with him, an invitation I declined due to my poor French. I was glad I had done so because free from any distractions about my French pronunciation I could experience the wonder of this sign of the unity of all men.

After the Mass and much handshaking with the congregation, the parish priest took me to his house for breakfast of coffee, bread, butter and jam and he marvelled at my appetite. He told me about the rapid decline in numbers coming to church in the last few years and how demoralized he had felt until he discovered the charismatic movement and recovered hope. He was a mild and encouraging enthusiast, not one of those fanatical charismatics whose gushing account of their own 'baptism in the spirit' implies that everyone else is still in exterior darkness. He offered me a hefty volume on charismatic prayer, but did not look shocked or offended by my lack of faith when I told him that I had to travel light and declined his gift.

In the afternoon I was well clear of Paris and spent three peaceful hours resting against a tree by the side of a stream, delighted at being in more open country at last. My delight was short lived. My route towards Melun should have been along back roads, but I misread the map in Combe le Ville and at 8 p. m. I was back in enemy territory on the main

73

N.5 with a continuous stream of traffic flowing from Fontaine-bleau towards Paris. After struggling for an hour, I found an earth track running parallel to the main road and spent another night on rocky hard ground.

Next morning in Melun I visited the church, did some shopping and was clear of the town and walking along the Seine by eleven. In my diary I noted that this was the hottest day so far, a note I was to repeat almost every day until I reached Grenoble. Three kilometres beyond Melun I called in at a cafe for a beer and then settled by the riverside for lunch and a long rest to make up the broken sleep of the last two nights. Before sleeping, I decided to write up my diary, which I had not touched since leaving Paris. I looked for my biro, a Papermate, which a friend had given me before I left Glasgow. It was not in any of the seven pockets of my jacket, nor in the rucksack, which I unpacked, nor in the long grass where I was sitting. Thinking I might have left it in the bar where I had the beer, I packed everything and returned to find it was not there. The heat aggravated my irritation at the loss but I began to reason with myself. Why get so worked up about the loss of a biro? So I started on my way along the Seine, resigned to life without a Papermate biro. Two kilometres further on I was questioning the value of this resignation. The biro was a gift, not just a biro, and I valued it because I valued the friendship which it expressed. It might have dropped out of my pocket when I was leaning over the fruit boxes in the grocer's shop in Melun. I ought to go back and look.

I returned to the grocer's shop and waited until 3.30 p. m. when it opened. I searched in vain. When I returned to the Seine, I suddenly realized I was no longer carrying my map folder, now lying in Melun church, the cafe, the grocer's or anywhere along the route. The maps and my schedule were of far more immediate importance than the biro. For a moment I felt alarm, not so much at this latest loss, but in fear at my own absent-mindedness. Perhaps I was suffering from sunstroke, my brain was no longer functioning and worse disasters would follow. I retraced my steps to the grocer who looked at me with pity this time and shrugged his shoulders despairingly like a man well schooled in the French philosophy of the absurd. I could not remember which bench I had occupied in the church so I searched them all without success. The cafe was equally unsuccessful.

For the third and, I hoped, last time I left Melun, snatched up my rucksack from the riverside bar as though it were to blame for all my misfortunes and stomped off along the path beside the river, hoping I could remember the map details I had studied that morning. My heels were beginning to hurt again and the pain started to spread through my body. I stumbled along in an agony of self-pity until I reached a private roadway by the river. On the right there were some beautiful old houses and gardens, each with its own private jetty on the river. I stopped by one of these jetties and dangled my feet in the Seine. In this way I recovered sufficient calm and energy to reach Bois-le-Roi where I bought some maps to replace those I had lost; I also bought a new biro. An excellent supper with a half-bottle of Côtes du Rhône compensated for the trials of the day. In the restaurant I learned that there was a campsite nearby. No feather mattress can compare with the comfort I experienced that night when I pitched my tent on soft grass after two nights on rock-hard surfaces.

In my meanderings around Melun I had walked 15 kilometres without getting any nearer to Rome. Next day, Tuesday, July 1, I hoped to walk 40 kilometres to make up for the lost time and distance. By 7 a. m. I was ready for the road, but the camp official who demanded my passport the night before did not open his office until nine. Eventually I was able to set off at a brisk pace. My heels which were so painful the day before were painless now and I felt I could walk for ever without tiring.

In Melun I had looked for a bank and was told that all banks are closed on Mondays. In Samois, a few kilometres from the campsite, I was told that Tuesday was their closing day. I spent the remainder of my money on food for lunch, preferring possible starvation to a return to Melun.

In the Forêt de Champagne I found a clearing with tables and benches set out under the trees. I can understand our pagan ancestors who worshipped the spirits of the forest. Especially when alone in them, I can experience changes of mood, which it is very easy to interpret as the mood of the forest, the voices of the trees. Forests of tall pine engender a very solemn, sombre stillness in the mind, grave elderly spirits, not given to frivolity. The Forêt de Champagne was very different. The bright sun and gentle breeze set the shadows dancing on the grass and the spirits were like children laughing in their play. They freed me for a moment to smile and laugh with them as I thought of my agitation of yesterday, running around like a clucking hen in search of my pen and maps, unable to laugh at the time.

Laughter is a grace, which takes us out of ourselves, a kind of ecstasy in which we seem to share in a mind which sees us in our ridiculous tininess and yet does not despise us but laughs in us and with us. 'One saith that laughter is the dance of the spirits, their freest motion in the harmony, and that the light of the heavens is the laughter of angels. Spiritual joy is the laughter of divine love, of the Eternal Spirit, which is love, in our spirits.' Those lines are from a seventeenth-century spiritual writer, a chaplain to Cromwell.

After lunch I sat on in the forest for two hours enjoying its peace. The aches and the pains, the tiredness and frustration of my experience in Melun and the worry it had caused me, the sights and the sounds, the peace of the evenings and the joy of the early morning, all came together in a sense of great happiness. I thought of the ancient Bernard, who had taken me shopping. He lived in the past, with his days of glory in Winchester as a military man, but he also lived fully in the present and so he was in no hurry. He seemed to enjoy each moment as it came, was interested in everyone and everything around him and wanted me to share it. I had enjoyed being with him, but my enjoyment was marred by my anxiety to be on the move, to get on with my plan to walk to Rome. Our whole life and character is contained in any incident, no matter how trivial it seems. In the peace of this forest I caught a glimpse of myself in the meeting with Bernard and I did not like it. A phrase came to my mind, *pas de violence*, which I had once heard from a spiritual director, who maintained that it was a basic principle of all spirituality, at a time when I much preferred Christ's text, 'The kingdom of heaven is taken by violence, and the violent bear it away,' interpreting it as meaning a vigorous determination in doing whatever I was doing. Failures made me reconsider this interpretation and slowly I am beginning to learn the wisdom of *pas de violence*.

'Don't do violence to yourself, don't force, don't coerce', was the message of that gentle director. Why not? Because 'the kingdom of God is like a mustard seed', something small, hidden, apparently insignificant and it is within us. Letting it grow is what spirituality is about. If we can find it and nurture it, we find a 'pearl beyond price' which we can then pursue with vigorous determination. The search leads us beyond ourselves to a new life, not only after death, but here and now. We cannot create the mustard seed, nor make it grow: we can only create the conditions favourable to its growth. But where is this mustard seed within us and how can we detect it? It is within all our inner experience, which we have to learn to listen to and interpret. Vigorous determination in carrying out plans and policies which ignore our inner experience can render us less capable of listening to it, and so stifle the mustard seed. So we have to be still sometimes, let our feelings and inner tensions speak to us and try to sift them.

At first we find a disordered jumble of emotions within us, base desires and high ideals, because there is a saint and a sinner within each of us. The high ideals may have nothing to do with religion as we understand it. They may come to us through our admiration of someone in fact or fiction because of their courage, love of truth, generosity, faithfulness, openness. These are the stirrings of the mustard seed, of the kingdom of God within us. He comes to each of us in our own individual way. The justification of all religious practice, of doctrines and disciplines, laws and regulations is that they can make us more perceptive and responsive to this gentle action of God within us, so that we let him have his say and discover that this way is really what we want most deeply. Religion which is presented in a threatening coercive manner,

77

which makes us afraid to consult our own feelings, and kills and stifles our spiritual growth, can lead to atheism in practice, although it is not explicitly expressed. That is why some forms of Catholic education, inflicted with threats of punishment both now and hereafter, can produce stifled or disillusioned men and women, while others, who profess no religion but have listened to their hearts, are more Christian in their behaviour than many of us who are practising Christians.

From the forest I walked to Champagne, found a bank and had the money to buy one glass. But I had a fair distance to walk to complete my 40 kilometres and champagne is a heady and with me a headachy drink. My route was along the river and canal paths at first and I did not tire until seven in the evening, when I reached the village of Dormelles, shopped for supper and began to look for a camping place. On the edge of the village were some bungalows with large open gardens behind them. I called at one of them and a nervous-looking woman answered and said she was sorry, but all the land behind the houses was private garden and no one could camp there. I wished her good evening and turned to go, when she said, 'Perhaps if you camp well down the bottom of the garden next door it will be all right. The owners are away at present.' After supper I noticed that several lights were on in the unoccupied house, and they were still on at five next morning when I started on my way. I realized that the poor woman had feared I might burgle it and must have turned the lights on as a deterrent. All the same I was thankful for my excellent camping site.

One of my most valuable possessions was a light, metal water-bottle which I always filled with drinking water whenever I started out in the morning and when it was running low I would call in at a house to have it filled. The morning I left Dormelles was exceptionally hot and after a few hours walking I called in at a farmhouse to have the bottle filled. The front door was ajar and I rang the bell, but there was no answer. I was on my way round to the back of the house when I saw a tap by the side of the wall. I filled the bottle from it and had just returned to put it in the rucksack when an elderly woman stuck her head out of a downstairs room and gave me an earful of rapid French. Sentence leaped after sentence, each more shrill than the last. It was not the kind of French I had learned at school. I listened in silence until the tirade was over and *Madame* recovered her breath. I explained that I was a Scot, that I had walked from London and was suffering from thirst in this delightful French weather. *Madame's* eyes popped in surprise. 'Then *Monsieur* will have need of wine,' she said. '*D'accord*,' I replied, pleased at being able to use this expression which peppered the conversation of the *routiers*. She poured out two glasses, passed one through the window, clinked glasses and we wished one another '*Santé*'. 'And what does *Monsieur* do apart from walking?' she asked. 'I am a Catholic priest,' I replied. The poor woman gulped. Intense fury had now given way to confusion and shame that she had spoken so rudely and had been so *sauvage* with a priest. I assured her that for all I had understood, she might have been hurling compliments at me and that all I would remember was her great kindness in offering me wine.

I usually rested in the afternoons because they were so hot and walked for two or three hours in the evening. By this stage of the walk I found six kilometres an hour a comfortable pace and began to think my walking problems were over. Two days later I wanted to abandon the journey.

I need no diary to remember Thursday, July 3. On the previous day I had walked too far in the heat, and my heels became very painful in the evening and were still tender after the first hour's walking next morning. I decided to walk through the afternoon so that I could end the day's walking around three, hoping that the long rest would give my heels time to recover. I wanted to walk from La Celle St Cyr to Senan, and took a short cut through a field track to a road, which I took to be the D.89 to Volgré. I was so sure of my map reading that I did not bother to check my direction by compass. After two hours walking in blistering heat, I ended up at Beon at 4.30 p. m., 1.5 kilometres from my starting point, where I drank a litre of beer, studied the map again and saw that there was a short cut through the forest to

Champvallon. The route looked simple enough and the barman confirmed this impression, sweeping his hand over a hill behind the village and assuring me the path was well marked. Refuelled with the beer, I decided to continue.

As I climbed the steep hill out of the village a tractor came up behind me and the driver offered me a lift. I remembered a passage in Belloc's *Path to Rome* where he was offered a lift in similar circumstances seventy-five years before. He had refused the lift but hung on to the back of the cart, and so was helped on his way while keeping his vow to use 'no wheeled thing', an action which led him on to discourse on the nature of vows. 'The essence of a vow', he wrote, 'is its literal meaning.' I thought his reasoning was false and an encouragement to idolatry, but I followed his example, clung to the back of the tractor and was greatly helped for two-thirds of the ascent until the tractor turned off into a clearing. I puffed and panted the rest of the way up the steep slope, the sudden surge of beer energy now running to waste in a lather of sweat. Near the summit, the forest path forked without any indication of the right path for Champvallon. My compass indicated the right hand fork, but after 2 kilometres it was leading me south-west instead of south-east. I left the path and made east through the thick forest. I took compass bearings every few metres, crackling my way through and muttering to myself as I had to step over dead branches and disengage my rucksack from live ones, all the time peering through salt-stung eyes for the next bearing.

At 7 p. m. I had reached the eastern edge of the forest and looked down on a vast plain stretching towards the south and showing tomorrow's route with Champvallon below me. Fortunately, there was a travelling grocer's van in the village and I was able to buy food for supper. Near the village the map showed a wood with a stream running through it. The stream turned out to be a thin trickle of grey water meandering between high nettles and a few scraggy trees.

The evening was warm and sultry. I pitched my tent hurriedly and prepared supper, but I was too tired to finish and crawled into the tent, leaving the flaps open because of the heat. I must have fallen asleep almost immediately for I was woken by a deafening clap of thunder and the sound of heavy rain on the tent. It was 3 a. m. and pitch dark in the moments between the lightning flashes. I felt a thud, sat up suddenly and found myself draped in drenched nylon. I groped for the torch, which was dead, then for my lighter, which was soaked, and in trying to remove the flint in order to dry it, I lost it in the waters splashing around the sleeping bag. Either I could lie in this sodden mass till dawn or I could try to pack the rucksack and move on. Packing the rucksack was not easy at the best of times. In the darkness with every article sodden, it seemed a hopeless task. I began with the sleeping bag, which had absorbed gallons of water. When I had rung it out and folded it, it felt like rolled lead. The rest of my possessions I folded up inside my cagoul and placed outside the tent, which I dismantled and packed in the rucksack on top of the sleeping bag. By this time, dawn was beginning to break. The packing completed, I could hardly lift the load on to my shoulders.

I was in a curiously detached mood when I left the wood and can remember wondering, after the nightmare of the last twenty-four hours, how far I would be able to walk before I collapsed from fatigue. The rain was still heavy and the sky a dull and uniform grey.

The first village I reached was still asleep and it was only after two hours walking that I found a place to stop. My reflections consisted largely of the utter stupidity of the whole undertaking to walk to Rome and of resolutions that I would never again act upon ideas thought up in the comfort of an armchair without a careful reckoning of the cost.

French villages begin life early. At 7 a. m. men were sitting at a café having their coffee and spirits. I ordered a coffee and 'whatever it is the *monsieurs* are having in those little glasses'. It was high octane and spread quickly through my body, coming out through my eyes and ears and setting my toes tingling. The next hour's walking was easy. The sky began to clear and at ten I was able to sit in the sun and partially dry out some of my clothes, lessening the weight I had to carry. I have never enjoyed the sun so much as at that moment, nor the smell of the woods and the earth after rain.

Romantic notions of the open-air life took over again. I was glad of the experience because subsequently, whenever I felt tired, I remembered it and muttered to myself those lines of Virgil, addressed by Aeneas to his discouraged troops, who had suffered yet another setback on their way from Troy to Rome: *O passi graviora, dabit deus his quoque finem*. (O you, who have endured far worse than this, know that God will put an end to these trials, too.)

A few hours later I was already muttering Virgil's lines. I was sure that I could find a hotel somewhere along the route, have a proper meal, book a room for the night and dry out my clothes and sleeping bag. It was 2.30 p. m. before I found a village; it had two restaurants but no hotel. The restaurants were very sorry, but they had finished serving lunches and all the shops were closed. I know a very placid man who says, 'When things get too much for me, I go to sleep,' so I slept in the sun just beyond the village and reached Chevannes around 5 p. m. hoping to find a room for the night. Chevannes does not cater for the tourist. I bought bread, pâté, cheese, fruit, condensed milk and cake and went in search of a camping place, leaving my rucksack and shopping in the village church.

Opposite the church there was a small farm, and an elderly man was sitting on the steps of the farmhouse kitchen. I asked if I might camp in his field for the night. After a minute's silence he spoke with an accent which I could not understand, but I caught the word *papiers*. 'Do you want to see my passport?' 'Yes.' I returned to the church to collect my rucksack and shopping and handed him the passport. His wife was then summoned and together they studied my passport page by page. At last I was accepted! 'You can camp here.' Once permission was granted they became very friendly, took me to the hen-run and watched me pitch the tent. I told them about last night's storm and showed them the sodden sleeping bag, hoping they might suggest drying it out in front of the kitchen fire, but they made no offer and so I hung the bag on a barn beam and slept without covering.

At 2 a. m., after three hours sleep, I awoke feeling fully rested. The night was clear and I walked around for a while

82

in the stillness which was broken only by the gentle splash of fish in a pond near my tent. After three days hard walking and very little sleep the night before, I thought I should be tired but felt wide awake. I was now beginning to experience a new freedom, freedom from my own self-conditioning which tells me when I should feel hungry and when I should feel tired. I discovered that my body was much more adaptable than my mind while I was walking, but the mind reasserted its control when I returned to 'normal' life.

There was a heavy mist when I started out next morning. When the sun broke through I was in a sheltered forest. At 3 p. m. I came to Mailly le Chateau, where I found a hotel opposite the thirteenth-century church. Ian Tweedie had advised me to stay at a hotel or *pension* at least once a week for a long rest and cooked meals. I followed his advice on this occasion, but did not feel the need of a hotel rest again until I was within two days of Rome.

For eighteen hours I lived the sybaritic life and enjoyed every minute of it. I washed and dried out all my clothes, including the sleeping bag, and started on the last 20 kilometres to Vézelay at 9.30 a. m. Although it was the hottest day so far, I was now walking easily along tracks and side-roads through most beautiful country and I did not tire until I was within a few kilometres of Vézelay. I called in at a cafe, where I sat with a group of French holidaymakers, who included in their number an earnest student of psychology with a sharp eye for any manifestation of abnormal behaviour. I was obviously an answer to a prayer, walking in mid-afternoon on the hottest day of a very hot summer with a 15.5–kilo pack on my back. After plying me with preliminary questions, she moved into the diagnosis. 'And are you walking alone?' 'Yes,' I said. 'Perhaps *Monsieur* prefers being alone to being with people', she suggested hopefully. 'No, I enjoy both being alone and being with people.' A shadow of disappointment swept across her face, but she was a determined student. 'I see,' she said after a pause, 'when you are alone you want to be with people, and when you are with people you want to be alone.' 'That is partly true,' I replied, 'solitude helps me to appreciate company and company helps me to appreciate solitude, but there's a time for speaking and a time for being silent.' She looked puzzled and disappointed and I was dismissed with a curt '*Bon voyage*'.

6

Vézelay

Vézelay rises high above the plain and had been visible for many miles before I reached the foot of the hill leading to the town with its famous romanesque basilica of St Mary Magdalene at the top. In the eleventh century the Benedictine abbey of Vézelay claimed to have the relics of Mary Magdalene, and the town became one of Europe's most famous pilgrimage centres, a stop *en route* for pilgrims from the north and east who were on their way to the shrine of St James at Compostella. It was also a rallying point for the crusaders, and a cross marks the spot where St Bernard preached the Second Crusade in 1146. Richard the Lion Heart and Philip II met there in 1190 before departing for the Third Crusade. St Thomas à Becket was in Vézelay when he excommunicated Henry II. The magnificent basilica was completed in the thirteenth century, when Vézelay fell into a decline because Provence claimed to possess better authenticated relics of Mary Magdalene.

Twentieth-century tourists filled the narrow streets on that Sunday afternoon. Near the top of the hill, just below the basilica, there is a *Pax Christi* hostel. *Pax Christi* is an international organization of Christians who work for the promotion of peace and understanding. They have branches throughout Europe and a centre in London. The hostel was manned during the summer by a multinational group of fourteen students – French, Dutch, German and Spanish – and could provide cheap accommodation for seventy people. Two Dutch students, Rita and Marie Thérèse, greeted me with a most welcome pot of tea and then took me to the basilica for an evening Mass.

Of all the cathedrals and basilicas I have seen, Vézelay is the most beautiful, very like Notre Dame in style, but lighter, more austere and less cluttered. What a monument to Christian hope! It was built by an anonymous architect in the thirteenth century in a town which had suffered bloodshed and disaster. In the twelfth century the abbey had become too wealthy and the people had risen in revolt, murdering the abbot. In the twelfth century, too, there had been a fire in Vézelay in which one thousand pilgrims died. Out of tragedy the basilica was built, its carvings over the main door recalling not 'the tears of things', but Christ in glory: not Christ the judge but Christ the redeemer and around him his apostles who were to preach his Gospel to all the nations of the world.

The evening Mass was one of my most memorable experiences of the whole pilgrimage. A Capuchin priest who looked like a picture of St Paul celebrated the Mass at a side altar for a group of seventy people. He seemed to mean every word he uttered and his eyes were kindly and still. The readings included St Paul's passage to the Romans, 'and if the Spirit of him who raised Jesus from the dead is living in you, then he who raised Jesus from the dead will give life to your own mortal bodies through his Spirit living in you'. The Gospel was Jesus' prayer in Matthew, 'I bless you, Father, Lord of heaven and earth, for hiding these things from the learned and the clever and revealing them to mere children.' When I heard those words I felt I had understood the meaning of the Hebrews' passage for the first time: 'The word of God is something alive and active; it cuts like any double-edged sword, but more finely: it can slip through the place where the soul is divided from the spirit, or the joints from the marrow.'

All the experiences of the walk so far, the pain and the pleasure, all the thought that had come to me, the life-memories, both sad and joyful, all the views of forests and plains, towns and cities, moments of peace and moments of agitation; all seemed to be gathered up in one blissful moment when my whole being delighted in the goodness of God. *Qu'il est bon, qu'il est bon, qu'il est bon, le bon Dieu!* I thanked him for the pilgrimage so far, that he had given me the health and strength to make this gesture, a walking, sometimes a tottering in search of him, because I was beginning to learn through this gesture that God is not at the end of the road but at the beginning of it, in every step of it, nearer to me than I am to myself. What does it profit a man if he gains the whole world and yet misses this truth?

The Capuchin priest recited the words of consecration over the bread, 'This is my body given up for you.' Life is the mysterious God of love communicating himself. The Mass is not an escape into a supernatural stratosphere but a plunging into the truth of life here and now, into the truth that God is with us and in us and that there are no depths of human suffering where he is not. Little children can understand the message but we become so learned and clever with our hideously complicated explanations of how the Eucharist 'works' that we can easily turn God's love into a complicated theological problem, 'thingyfying' the Eucharist. I sometimes wonder if Christ would have understood our explanations.

After Mass I met all the other members of the student group at *Pax Christi* and we had a marvellous meal with conversation in a mixture of English, French and German. The youngest in the group, known as *la petite*, was a highly intelligent sixteen-year-old, who fired the most impossibly difficult questions at us all on the meaning of faith. It was not an anguished conversation. They were a laughing, happy group whose faith demanded understanding. We retired late and I found I could not sleep, partly because of the heat and partly because I did not feel tired enough. I stayed up writing, slept for a few hours and then went to the basilica in the early morning.

On Monday the students asked me to say Mass for them in the hostel sometime in the evening after a group of fifty American students were due to arrive. In the afternoon I went up to my room to prepare something for the international Mass. It was siesta time, the shops were shut and the streets outside were unusually quiet. Suddenly the silence was shattered by Yorkshire voices in the street below. 'Pax bloody Christi it says on door an' all welcoom.' 'Thur's six burds in yon front room,' said another voice, 'coom on an' we'll chat 'em oop.' 'Looks like a religious set-oop ta me,' said a third, 'let's go and 'ave soom beer.' 'Bloody awful French beer,' said the first speaker, adding, '*le chat est sur le mur*, that's t'only bit of French I remember. Up Leeds United.' And the descendants of the English crusaders went their way.

When the fifty American students arrived, we told them that we were having Mass after supper and that they were welcome to join us and contribute some prayers and songs in English. I had taken it for granted that they were a Catholic group and it was only after they had accepted the invitation that I learned they were, in fact, an intensely serious group of fundamentalist Protestant Evangelicals whose fore-fathers would be tossing around in their graves at the thought of their children attending Roman Catholic idolatrous worship. These children of the twentieth century seemed to have no scruple. They each had a copy of the Bible together with a booklet composed by their professor containing excerpts from Europe's literary gems from Homer, through Virgil and up to Solzhenitsyn, with an appendix containing prayers and hymns.

Most of them joined in the Mass; they chose some of the readings, commented on them, sang 'Amazing Grace', and when they joined in the prayers of intercession, I thought we would not finish Mass before dawn. It was a most catholic Eucharist, in its literal sense, international and interdenominational. I said the Mass in French with an English commentary and we had prayers and songs in five languages, a great experience for all of us of Christ's power to unite us across the barriers of language and expression of belief. When Christ is our bond and our peace, then our differences are no longer barriers to communication, and we become grateful for our diversity in unity. The Mass evoked in me nostalgic memories of Masses at Turnbull Hall, where various denominations and races prayed together and we could experience his power to rid us of our fears of each other and make us grateful to him for such a varied world.

As the weather was so hot, I decided to leave Vézelay at 3

a. m. on the Tuesday, hoping to have completed 32 kilometres before the sun made walking impossibly tiring. I told the students of my plan and said goodbye the night before. When I eventually came down the stairs at 4.30 a. m., having slept in, I found two of the students sleeping in camp beds across the front door to ensure that I could not get out before they had made me breakfast. Marie Thérèse and Rita had stayed up till 3 a. m., but could not keep awake and left me a note wishing me *bon voyage*.

I felt very sad as I walked down the hill leaving Vézelay behind and I would gladly have spent a few more days in such excellent company, but the pilgrim, if he is ever to reach his destination, has to be detached. During the day I kept thinking about the meaning of being a pilgrim and of the pilgrim nature of the Church.

The Second Vatican Council spoke of the Church as 'the pilgrim people of God', reminding us of a very ancient traditional description, which goes back to Abraham, who was called to leave his own country and become a wanderer, a searcher. Those within the Church who dislike change and oppose it in the name of tradition are not within the tradition of the Church, which, by its very nature, must be a Church on the move, a searching Church without any abiding city here. She betrays herself if she stops searching, settles down and thinks she has arrived. There is something essentially provisional about the Church, because she is a people led by the Spirit of the transcendent God, who cannot be enclosed in definitions nor in temples made by human hands.

Pilgrims must travel light, otherwise they cannot continue on their way. Their equipment is designed for the journey and they do not fill their rucksacks with unnecessary possessions which only slow them down. As they walk they discover other treasures, which no one can take from them: an inner peace, new ways of seeing, a delight in nature. It is because they are on the move that they make new discoveries and because they do not possess that they are able to enjoy everything.

When we stop, there is always the temptation to settle down to stay, prolong the rest, enjoy the company for longer.

We may never meet again, so why not linger? We begin to feel at one with these new friends. Yet when we do leave them, we do so knowing that this oneness can never be broken. All meetings contain an eternal element in them. We part the richer for having met each other and nothing, neither physical distance nor even death, can rob us of that gift because we are one in Christ, even with those who do not believe in Christ. They may not know him by name, or they may not be able to see beyond the institutions which bear his name and which may repel them.

The pilgrim wants them to break through the surface of their feelings and impressions and experience this longing to be at one with self and with all creation. This is not something we shall ever achieve, because the more we experience it, the more we know there is to experience and the further we want to go. Everything in life – food, drink, sleep, thought, work, above all friendship – they are all steps on this road to at-oneness with our own being, with every other human being, with all creation, a wanting to be dissolved and to be within the heart of it all. 'Unless you lose your life you cannot find it.'

If we are to be pilgrims, then we must want this at-oneness more than anything else, and if we really want it, our lives will be characterized by openness and adaptability. If we are led by the mysterious God, our lives will be anchored in only one certainty, that we are mysteriously called beyond ourselves. The certainty of this faith will be the opposite of dogmatism. Our faith in God will make us sceptical of any once-for-all formulation of our faith because our faith teaches us that God is the God of surprises, who will always be mystery for us.

The justification of Christian doctrines and definitions is that they can help to keep the mystery open. Christian doctrine does not claim (although it is often mistakenly thought to do so) to give us adequate descriptions of God or of his Church. Doctrine is offered to us to help us keep on the track of mystery, to help us to continue searching. Heretical doctrine is teaching which leads us down a cul-de-sac, diverting us from the path which leads into mystery.

Pilgrims of the past have recorded their experience of God and those records are presented to us, especially those records called the Bible, not as a substitution for our own experience but to help us to recognize its meaning. The words of Scripture are given to us to help us recognize what is happening within us. 'The word of God is something alive and active, it can judge the secret emotions and thoughts.' We must not block these words with our own dogmatism. We must be still before them, emptying our mind of its preconceived notions. 'Unless you become as little children, you cannot enter the kingdom of God.'

God calls all men, loves all men. The Church is the gathering of those who are aware of their call by God and who meet to celebrate that awareness. They know that God is calling all men and that many who have never heard of the Church may, in fact, be much nearer to God than they are. This is not a reason for regret, but for thanking God in his goodness. It is also a reason for listening carefully and learning from men who profess no religion.

Those who profess faith in God, who experience his mysterious call within them, form a restless people in search of a way, the way of at-oneness. They will be joyful people, who have found a direction and want to communicate it, sing of it, tell everyone about it, because the unity they experience is a summons to greater unity. They will be a gentle people, tolerant, not preoccupied about possessions, because they are in search of the only possession that matters and which no one can take from them. They are not worried about social status and prestige, because they have found a security within themselves which nothing can destroy; nor are they afraid of being challenged, because they know how little knowledge they have, and welcome every challenge as an opportunity to learn.

Ideally, the Church is a pilgrim people, blissfully happy in their indifference to wealth and possessions, unworried by the insecurity of all systems and institutions because they know they have no abiding city here. They are *en route*, a learning people, always ready to admit their errors in the face of truth,

91

welcoming the truth wherever it is found and knowing that it can be found among all people, whether Christian or not.

What a marvellous Church that would be! There are individuals and groups within the Roman Catholic Church who show these characteristics and qualities, but they are exceptions. To the outsider, and to many within the Catholic Church, far from appearing to be a pilgrim Church, a Church on the move, she gives the impression of being a Church which has found its destination, discovered all the answers and has now settled down to await the day when everyone will recognize its truth. New ideas are treated with suspicion, not welcomed. It is as though the pilgrim had accumulated too many possessions on the way, found the weight too heavy to carry and so settled down to look after and protect the overloaded rucksack. The pilgrim Church became the settled Church, the static Church. The pilgrim people, unable to cope with marauding bands, settled down to protect themselves, threw up stockades, then high walls. The pilgrim Church became the parade-ground Church, the beleaguered garrison of Christ the King. Within its high walls the loyal troops performed their outmoded arms drill and manoeuvres in the parade-ground, assured that as long as they kept up the drill and obeyed orders unquestioningly, they could be sure of ultimate victory. If they disobeyed regulations and failed to defend the bastions, then they would be shot down for all eternity by their commander-in-chief.

'That is a ridiculous caricature and it is irresponsible and disloyal for any Catholic, most of all for a Catholic priest, to write in this way.' I know that it is a caricature. If I thought it were the whole truth, I should have leaped over the barrack walls years ago. It is because I know that it is not the whole truth and because I can find pilgrim qualities within the Catholic Church that I stay within her and am most grateful to be a member. But the caricature is true in so far as it describes the impression which the Catholic Church gives to many non-Catholics and the ways in which we are all liable to behave within the Church.

Taizé: a Sign of Hope

I left Vézelay at 5.30 a. m. as the delicate mist in the plains below was rising to the touch of the morning sun and walked briskly but easily through wooded, rolling countryside. After 13 kilometres I looked back and could see the hill of Vézelay to the north.

My thoughts on the pilgrim nature of the Church had left me not in a state of depression, but with a strange heaviness of heart, which I could neither identify nor shake off at first. I believed the Church should be the pilgrim Church, on the move, detached from possessions, prestige, influence, because it is attached to her Lord, characterized by a folly which is wiser than human wisdom and a weakness stronger than human strength. I wanted to share in this life of the Church. The heaviness which I experienced was in seeing the gulf which separated what I really was from what I wanted to be.

I was sorry at leaving Vézelay and the students. I had experienced at-oneness with them and when I left them I knew that this oneness could never be broken. I was the richer for having met them and, hopefully, they were the richer for having met me. I knew all this and yet I felt heavy and dispirited. The heaviness, I realized later, was not at leaving Vézelay, nor even at the far greater wrench of leaving Glasgow, but at the whole pattern of my life as a Jesuit.

Part of me longs for permanence: the stability of life in one place with a fixed circle of friends. Sometimes, as I walked past the small farms and saw the farmer and his family working in the fields, I would feel a pang of loneliness and envy. As a Jesuit, there is no certainty of permanence in one community, one place, one job. Ignatius has it in the Rule:

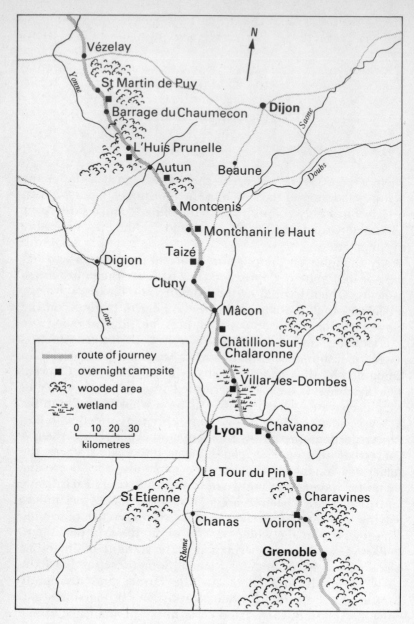

N

Vézelay

Yonne

St Martin de Puy

Barrage du Chaumecon

Dijon

Saône

L'Huis Prunelle

Autun

Beaune

Doubs

Montcenis

Montchanir le Haut

Digion

Taizé

Cluny

Loire

Mâcon

Châtillion-sur-Chalaronne

Villar-les-Dombes

route of journey

overnight campsite

wooded area

wetland

0 10 20 30
kilometres

Lyon

Chavanoz

La Tour du Pin

Charavines

St Etienne

Chanas

Voiron

Rhône

Grenoble

Vézelay to Grenoble

'Our vocation is to travel to various places,' wherever there is work to be done, wherever superiors may send us. Jesuit superiors today are very humane, at least I have always found them so, and they are unlikely to uproot us from a place we like and set us down in another to which we are totally unsuited. On the other hand, if we dig ourselves into a particular place and make it quite clear that no power on earth is going to move us, we may be comfortable, stable and secure, but our lives as Jesuits no longer make sense. I want to remain a Jesuit, and therefore have to come to terms with frequent uprooting. While it is true that we part the richer for having met each other and that nothing, neither physical distance nor even death can rob us of that gift, it is also true that at each parting we feel as though we have lost something of ourselves. This uprooting from friends, familiar surroundings, from the work which has become part of us, is a painful process and can be very destructive. The temptation is to deaden the feelings in order to cope with the pain and it was fear of this temptation which was at the root of the heaviness of heart I was now experiencing.

If we stifle our feelings, we can then accept change more easily but at the cost of our humanity, our sensitivity, our very selves, which is what 'the soul' means. 'What does it profit a man if he gains the whole world and suffers the loss of his own soul?' What does it profit someone to become a 'damned good religious', but without feeling, a perfect organization person, dead before death? Such a person may be thought to be a model of selflessness, indifference, obedience, but is dead. I began to understand Paul's famous passage more clearly· 'If I give away all that I possess piece by piece, and if I even let them take my body to burn it, but am without love, it will do me no good whatever.'

I found myself praying for a full life in pain rather than a half life in peace. It was only later that I realized this was not what I wanted either. Salvation is neither in suffering pain nor in enjoying security, but lies only in the free gift of God's love, communicated to us and expressing itself in patience and kindness, in delight in the truth and readiness 'to excuse, to trust, to hope and endure whatever comes'.

95

The sun was too strong for afternoon walking and I spent four hours resting in the woods above the village of St Martin de Puy, where my heaviness lifted. The map indicated several beauty spots along the route I was to take in the evening to the north of the Barrage de Chaumecon, a lake about 4 kilometres in length. The wooded road was very steep at first, climbing to about 450 metres and levelling out to reveal the beauty spots, which had been turned into rubbish dumps, a depressing sight.

I was tiring quickly, and my feet were beginning to hurt and so absorbed my attention that I took a wrong turning and found myself walking along the east side of the lake instead of the west. The route along the east side climbed steeply above the lake with thick forest on either side and no sign of a clearing. My feet were very painful by now, as though the tendons on the soles had crossed and tangled with each other, sending sharp pains down the toes, something I had not experienced since the first days after leaving Weybridge. There was a waterfall by the side of the road with just enough space around it to pitch the inner tent. The ground was soft, sandy and damp, but I slept soundly on it and did not start out again until 9 a. m., through open country at first and then into the Bois de Montsauche.

By 2 p. m. I had covered 25 kilometres and was just going to stop for a rest when I saw a man, woman and small girl camping in a field. I hailed them and passed on. The man came out after me and invited me to join them. The little girl was very shy at first and sat reading an illustrated book on animals, but she soon put it down and studied me in silence. 'She is very interested in all kinds of animals,' said *maman*. She continued to study me as we drank coffee and liqueurs, all the while exchanging life-histories. Just as I was leaving, the little girl spoke. 'Is it carrying a weight that has made *monsieur* so thin?' she asked her mother.

As I was passing through the forest I had seen a number of signs saying *Sangliers* and *Pièges*, but could not remember the meaning of either word. The signs usually appeared where there was a forest clearing. *Sangliers* sounded a bloodthirsty word, but I liked the sound of *Pièges* and took it to mean 'new plantations'. Later that evening I looked up both words in the pocket dictionary to discover that *sanglier* means 'wild boar' and *piège* means 'trap': useful information for my route next day through the Forêt d'Anôst.

That evening, just before entering the forest, I passed through a village where an old man was at work on his garden. I asked him if he could recommend a place where I might camp for the night. 'Why not camp here?' he asked, pointing to his front garden. Having led me into it and introduced me to his next-door neighbours across the fence, he then took me on a tour of his vegetable garden at the back, showed me the fresh water tank and wished me a good night. Although I had walked for more than 32 kilometres, I was not tired and my feet had not hurt all day. I had some wine, wrote a few letters and had just started preparing supper when *monsieur* appeared, clad in blue-striped pyjamas, puffing his pipe and bearing in one hand a huge bowl of strawberries and in the other a bowl of sugar. He told me that his son had been keen on camping and was always hungry. He apologized for his strawberries because they had too much rain in the spring. They tasted excellent to me, right down to the last bite.

So that I could have plenty of time to visit Autun 32 kilometres away I was on my way through the shady Forêt d'Anôst by 6 a. m. the next day. The road was lined with walls of felled trees and the air was scented with resin, and walking was easy until I joined the main road. The traffic was heavy and there was no shade from the merciless sun. I forced the pace hoping to make Autun before 1 p. m., reached the edge of the city in time, but was in no state to go anywhere for a meal. I washed and changed in a garage before finding a *restaurant des routiers* for lunch. They had finished serving. I ordered a beer and asked to have my flask filled with drinking water. I was charged as much for the water as for the beer. When I left the restaurant I was tired, hungry and ill-tempered, with no inclination to look at cathedrals, however famous. I lay by the river bank, ate some bread and cheese and drank the costly water. I tried to sleep but there was no shade and the sun was at its hottest. Finally, I climbed the hill into the city, found a cafe where I sat writing postcards, which I subsequently lost, ate ice cream and drank lemonade. I was on the second lemonade when the absurdity of my mood struck me. I was five years old again, hot and cantankerous and not even ice cream could cure me.

By 5 p. m. I had summoned the energy to find the famous cathedral. It was mercifully cool now and I sat down to rest before examining it in detail. An hour and a half later I awoke, my neck very stiff from leaning over in sleep. Since I had hardly eaten all day and wanted to be well clear of Autun before camping for the night, I made a lightning tour of the cathedral and then headed for the Forêt de Planoise, confident that I could find some place to eat before camping for the night. At the edge of the forest I found a cafe where *madame* gave me an enormous meal of salad, pâté, omelette, the most grizzly, salty ham I have ever tasted, cheese, fruit, bread and a carafe of wine. '*Monsieur* has a very good appetite,' she said at the end of the meal. As *monsieur* had walked 40 kilometres in the heat and eaten very little, it was not surprising. I started walking again, a very steep climb into the forest, parched with thirst, soaking with sweat and half-asleep from fatigue. I camped at the first stretch of grass I could find, dangerously near the road, and slept for ten hours in spite of the traffic which must have been passing.

After *madame's* meal and the ten hours sleep, the next day's walking was easy through the forest to Montchanir le Haut. It had been cooler all day and there was thunder in the air as I approached the town. The sky darkened and I felt the first drops of rain.

I felt my first moment of real fear that evening. When the rain began I asked a man if he knew of any place nearby where I could camp for the night. He was just getting into his car and told me that he could take me back a kilometre to the Étang Berthaud, just south of the town, where I could camp in peace by the lakeside, but he warned me that I should camp well away from the road in case the police caught me.

I found a spot out of sight of the main road, had a quick supper and crawled into my tent just as heavy rain was beginning. It was a very isolated place, still and quiet once the rain had stopped. At 2 a. m. I awoke suddenly and felt unaccountably afraid, for I have often slept peacefully in lonely places without fear. I was in the stage between sleep and wakefulness when it is difficult to distinguish dreams from reality and so I could not tell whether the sound of a motorcycle approaching was reality or my imagination. Why had that man been so insistent that I camp well out of sight of the main road? There was no doubt now. It was a motor-cycle and it was slowing down and stopped some distance from my tent. I heard quiet voices of men approaching. My only weapon was my penknife, but I had no chance of finding it quickly in the dark. I could try to pull out the tent-pole behind my head the moment they attacked and use it as a weapon, but then I realized I would not have the leverage, lying as I was on my back, to wrench the pole free from its many ground-pegs. The voices were fainter now. Perhaps they had planned a simultaneous attack from front and rear. I lay waiting for the moment of truth when I heard another motorcycle, more voices and then silence. And so it continued at intervals through the hours of darkness. I emerged from the tent as dawn was breaking to find forty peaceful French-men fishing by the lakeside. The 'terrorists' wished me *bon voyage* as I left the lake to walk the 10 kilometres to Taizé.

It was a beautiful route through lanes and byways, but the heat was intense and although I passed through many villages, I could find no shops. At lunchtime I called in at a farmhouse to ask where I could buy food. The family were sitting down to lunch and I could not keep my eyes off the table. 'You'll find shops at Taizé,' they told me, 'twelve kilometres further on,' whereupon they started on their meal. In a field I tried to rest, but it seemed to be holding a national gathering of French insects, including some vicious relatives of the horsefly, and the energy I used in trying to defend myself would have been better spent in walking.

In the distance I could see Taizé, which, like Vézelay, is set on a hill. Despite the afternoon heat I struggled on, so that by the time I reached the main road within 5 kilometres of Taizé, I was so exhausted that I was falling asleep as I walked. I lay down by the verge for a nap, but hooting lorries gave me no peace. Below the village of Taizé there are two hotels and in one of them I had my first meal of the day. I climbed the hill to the village. The first impression was that I had walked into a gypsy encampment. The fields on either side of the road were lined with tents, large brown army tents on one side, private tents and caravans on the other and there were hundreds of youngsters wandering about.

I wanted to visit Taizé as an unprejudiced, objective observer. I had read about Roger Schutz, a Protestant minister, whose studies in the history of Christianity had convinced him of the need for a revival of the monastic tradition in Protestantism. In 1940 he gathered a group about him, settled in Taizé, where he gave shelter to Jews and other refugees until the Germans took over Vichy, and he had to return to Geneva. In 1944 he returned to Taizé and today the monastery numbers more than 70 monks, representatives of many Christian denominations of the Reformed, Orthodox and Roman Catholic Churches. The Rule of Taizé is a masterpiece of simplicity and fidelity to the gospel, and Roger Schutz' *Letters from Taizé* are marked by that same simplicity. His message is that Christ calls all men, irrespective of race, creed or social status and calls us all into his unity and peace.

Besides my reading, I had met two of the monks of Taizé who had come to Scotland a few years before and had taken part in ecumenical services during the Octave of Church Unity. One of the meetings, which I attended was a particularly stormy one, and I was impressed by the calm and simplicity of Brother Thomas, a Church of Scotland minister and now a monk of Taizé. As he began to address the congregation in St Mary's Episcopal Cathedral in Glasgow, the meeting was disrupted by a certain Pastor Glass and his followers who were scattered throughout the congregation and felt called to warn all present that 'Rome is Antichrist, the Whore of Babylon' and that 'the Mass is a Roman idolatry'. Eventually the police were called in and the pastor and his men hustled out of the cathedral. At the end of the service they were still standing about in groups on the pavement outside holding their banners aloft. A Church of Scotland

woman whom I knew, took me by the arm and said, 'I feel
very bad about the police being called in. Come and say good
evening to the pastor.' She was a strong-minded woman as
well as being a very kind one, and so I obeyed. The pastor
was charming, shook hands and said to me, 'You know, you
and I have more in common with each other than that lot,'
pointing in the general direction of the cathedral. 'What
would you say we have in common?' I asked. 'You believe in
the Pope,' he said, 'and I believe in the Scripture, but that
lot don't believe in anything at all.' I was just beginning to
make a few distinctions when one of the pastor's men bearing
a standard warning against the Whore of Babylon interrupted
with 'The Mass is an eleventh-century invention.' This
distracted me from the Scripture-Tradition problem, which
had been my main interest during four years study of
theology, and made me turn to the history of the Eucharist,
but at this point a policeman arrived asking us to 'Move
along please'. We parted with handshakes and smiles. The
standard-bearer had the last word. 'Goodnight, Father,' he
said.

It was funny: it was also tragic. The pastor and his men
were simple people, convinced of the rightness of their cause,
and opposition to their ideas only made them the more
convinced that they were fighting with the God of righteousness on their side. It is very easy for the rest of us to sit back
and say, 'Aren't they impossible!' and fail to recognize the
bigotry in our own attitude. If we really cared about them
we would set out to win them with kindness. For years I had
been interested in ecumenism, had read numerous books,
attended conferences and taken part in ecumenical services.
All these activities were useful, but they did not excite me. I
was much more moved by informal meetings with Christians
of other denominations when we talked, worked and prayed
together. Then I knew that work for unity among Christians
is not a sideline for churchmen without any other serious
occupation, but is an essential of the faith and mission of the
Church. It is not a branch of church activity, but must be
the spirit in all our activity. I saw too that, while lip service
is paid to ecumenism, action showed indifference or hostility,

obscured by such phrases as, 'We must not upset the simple faith of our people', or, 'The time is not right yet, we must hurry slowly'. Here at Taizé, thousands of people from all Christian denominations gathered, the numbers increasing every year. But although I wanted to be objective about Taizé, I could not get rid of certain misgivings.

While in Glasgow, I had met many students who had visited Taizé, and the enthusiasm of some of them on their return bordered on fanaticism. They were oozing ecumenical love and peace from every pore, wanted to abandon their studies and instead travel the world spreading the Good News. I used to tell them that there was a lifetime's work under their very noses in Scotland. On being asked how they would set about preaching this message of love and peace, they would wave their arms about, pepper every statement with 'You know what I mean' and 'It kind-of happens', and then grow irritable when I said that I did not know what they meant, nor what 'It' was, nor how 'kind of' qualifies 'happens'.

My first hour did nothing to win me to Taizé. I stood in a queue with hundreds of rucksack-bearing youths while student officials, full of jolly backslapping inefficiency, joked among themselves and kept us waiting, presumably until 'it kind of happened'. I was very far from a 'we are all jolly Christians together' kind of mood. I had just walked 40 kilometres in the heat and my thoughts were rather on the Gulag Archipelago. Eventually, I shuffled past a table, paid 19 francs for camping and meals until Monday morning together with a subscription to the *Taizé Newsletter* and was shown a corner of the field next to the army tents where I could camp for the night. A man approached in the half-dark and offered to help me pitch the tent. He was an enthusiastic but unskilled helper who tangled the ropes, dug the pegs deep in the wrong places and produced what could be aptly termed 'a kind of happening'. Fortunately, I was tired beyond irritability. Next day, I came to know my helper in the daylight. He was a generous and gentle character, a recovered alcoholic.

Later that evening I visited the chapel, which had been built for the monks by an international team of young volunteers from the German Reconciliation Movement and completed in 1962. A few years ago the back wall of the church was removed to accommodate the increasing numbers of visitors and was replaced by a spacious canopy, a typical Taizé gesture. Inside, the stained glass windows give a restful light, a matted carpet emphasizes the silence and there are no fixed chairs or kneelers, which gives an impression of great spaciousness. Stacking chairs are provided at the back for those who cannot pray comfortably prostrate, kneeling, or in the lotus position.

Next day I attended morning prayer in the chapel with a thousand other people. It was a very simple service of psalms, readings and periods of silence. Afterwards, we queued in the hot sun for breakfast among a babel of voices – European, Asian, Indian, African, English, waiting for a cup of hot chocolate and two pieces of bread and butter. At eleven there was a Eucharist attended by about 3,000 people, which I thought an enormous number, but I was told that at Easter and Whitsun 40,000 would gather there. The congregation took up various postures. Older members gravitated to the chairs at the back. The monks, dressed in white habits, entered, not in procession, but in their own time, and took their places with the laity around the altar.

As there were so many young people present, I expected and feared a noisy liturgy with folksy hymns and 'with-it' prayers but my fears were unfounded. The stillness in the vast gathering before the Eucharist began was remarkable. The service began with short readings from Scripture in a variety of languages, some very simple psalm singing and many silent pauses for private prayer. There was no sermon, no word of explanation of the service, which was allowed to speak for itself. A large number of people, young and old, representing the various nations present, filed up to the altar at the offertory bearing the gifts of bread and wine, fruit of the earth and work of human hands, symbols of all that we have and are. After presenting the gifts to the celebrant, the people stood with the monks around the altar, a sign that we all, clerical and lay, share in the priesthood of Christ and celebrate the Eucharist together.

The prayers used on this occasion were taken from one of the Roman Canons and began with the eucharistic prayer of praise. 'It is indeed right and fitting, it is our duty and leads to our salvation that we should thank you always and everywhere, Lord, Holy Father, almighty and eternal God, through Christ, who is our Lord . . . Holy, Holy, Holy Lord God of hosts. Heaven and earth are full of your glory, Hosanna in the highest . . . And so Father, we bring you these gifts. We ask you to make them holy by the power of your Spirit, that they may become the body and blood of your Son, our Lord Jesus Christ, at whose command we celebrate this Eucharist.' The celebrant took the bread in his hands and said those words of Christ, his gift to mankind: 'Take this, all of you, and eat it: this is my body which will be given up for you.' Together we recited the Our Father: Europeans, Asians, Africans, Indians, Americans, South Americans, English, Scots and Irish, the family of man, children before God. 'May the peace of Christ be with you always,' said the celebrant, and we turned to wish each other the peace of Christ, which can break down the barriers of fear and mistrust which separate us from one another. The monks mingled with the people and I spotted Roger Schutz, because he was the last to return to the altar, as though he wanted to wish every individual the peace of Christ.

At communion time the monks came down among the people in pairs, one holding the plate with consecrated bread and the other with the chalice. After holy communion there was a long period of silence. In one sense it was a very ordinary, traditional liturgy; but it was celebrated with a peace and reverence which helped me to understand the ravings of student Taizé enthusiasts. 'It kind of happens.' It is the experience of Christ's real presence in me and in those around me, a presence which takes us up in our differences and draws us into a unity which does not obliterate the differences but makes us grateful for them, because they enrich the unity. In Christ I can be at one with my brother and sister Presbyterian, Methodist, Anglican, Asian, African, Indian, American. 'It' calls me beyond myself, beyond the limits of my national and religious prejudice, to discover a new unity with all creation. Because of 'It' I can go out and find that all creation is transformed. The sun, the clouds, the trees are still the same, but their meaning is different. 'The world is charged with the grandeur of God,' as Gerard Manley Hopkins wrote. The God in whom all things live and have their being has given himself to us under the sign of bread, and tells us to love one another as he has loved us. 'It sort of happens' because it is something too great to be the product of human ingenuity: it is grace which is gratuitous, freely given.

Every Christian Church believes this. Why then are most of them falling down and empty, apart from a few elderly faithful, while Taizé, situated in a remote part of France, cannot accommodate its numbers, especially the young? The answer, I think, lies in the simplicity of Taizé. God loves and welcomes all men, coerces none. The monks believe this and become, in St Paul's words, 'the goodness of God'. When this goodness is manifest, it attracts men. Taizé is a living proof of this truth. I have attended many meetings on pastoral work when the same wrong questions are asked: 'Why are so few people interested in religion any more and have given up church-going?' It is a false question, because people are interested in religion, but not in the kind of religion which does not touch our deeper longings. The false question inevitably produces the same monotonous false answer: 'It is because of the materialism and permissiveness of our twentieth century and the general deterioration in moral standards'; a comfortable answer for the clergy because it demands nothing from us except moral disapproval at which we excel. A truer answer to the question 'Why do people no longer come to Church?' is 'Because they can no longer recognize in it the breadth of Christ's love'. When they do see it, they flock in, as at Taizé.

During the morning Eucharist I had prayed for Christian unity, especially Catholic-Protestant unity in Northern Ireland and in the West of Scotland. In Glasgow I had been constantly surprised at the mutual ignorance and mistrust between Catholics and Protestants and I had seen something of the damage it can do. In the Taizé chapel that morning, when we celebrated our unity with Christ and with one

105

another, I could not help thinking of the bigotry which can also be fostered in his name; bigotry which leads us to justify our selfishness, our narrowness, our greed for power and prestige, by appealing to the 'faith of our fathers', whether Catholic or Protestant. I thought of the recently built school in the West of Scotland, which had been divided into two completely separate sections under the same roof, so that Catholic and Protestant children could learn separately, uncontaminated by one another's presence. Even the playground had been partitioned by a huge fence to keep the very footballs apart. The only hint of ecumenism was in the common boiler, which heated Catholics and Protestants alike. Whatever arguments there may be for separate Catholic schools, they have to be balanced against the truth that there is no more certain recipe for fostering mutual ignorance and mistrust, and consequently undermining the very essence of Christianity than to keep people in close physical proximity but discourage them from communicating.

In the evening I met Brother Thomas again. I was very anxious to know how he, a Church of Scotland minister, had become a monk of Taizé, and how he now felt about the religious divisions in his native Scotland. He talked about his life at Taizé, his work with the groups who visited the place, his work with the Council of Youth begun at Taizé and now spread throughout the world. He had not forgotten Scotland, but he felt his work was here. On Catholic-Protestant relations in Scotland his only comment was: 'Why are they so afraid of one another?' I suggested that a Taizé community in Scotland might help us to be less afraid. We then chatted about various common acquaintances and friends, including Rev. Colin Douglas who had been assistant chaplain at Glasgow University and was now a minister in Airdrie; he and Brother Thomas had studied together. Colin wanted to accompany me on the walk to Rome, but he could not get time off to do the whole journey and so had planned to meet me at Grenoble and accompany me over the Alps to the Mediterranean.

I spent the rest of the evening chatting to various groups from France, Holland and England about their impressions of Taizé. Some commentators attribute its phenomenal growth to the personality of the Prior, Roger Schutz. I do not know of any movement within the Christian Church which cannot be attributed to the gifts of an individual – Peter, Paul, Benedict, Augustine, Francis, Dominic, Luther, Calvin, Ignatius. There are some who go on to make the gloomy prediction that Taizé will collapse when Roger Schutz dies. All that I have read and the little I saw contradicts this gloomy prophecy. Taizé communicates Christ's welcome to all men. Visitors are not proselytised, coerced or threatened, but given a glimpse of what they can become in Christ and an opportunity to meet, reflect and pray together on the meaning of their lives. If the work of Taizé is of God, it will survive. The monks know this and so they are not as worried about the future as some of the commentators. A few kilometres down the road stand the ruins of Cluny, once the spiritual powerhouse of Europe, now transformed in part into a national stud, a sober reminder of transitoriness. At Taizé there are few permanent buildings. The majority of visitors live in tents, an excellent reminder of the pilgrim nature of the Church.

As I left on Monday morning at 5.30, the sun was coming up over the orange-coloured rim of the horizon. Already there were a few people in the chapel. I prayed for Taizé, its community and work, for the Councils of Youth and especially for Glasgow, and I thanked God for the hope which Taizé gives us.

It was a short walk down the valley to Cluny, where I spent most of the day. The monastery of Cluny, founded in 909, became the most important spiritual centre of Europe with an abbey church which rivalled St Peter's in Rome. Today, little remains of its past glory. After 200 years of remarkable abbots and rapid growth (there were 1,184 Cluniac houses and over 10,000 monks spread from England to Poland), Cluny went into decline. After the French Revolution the great abbey was dismantled and its stones sold. Only the south arm of the west transept remains today.

Later I visited the monastery library and asked the librarian if the library included any accounts of the frequent journeys which many of the abbots made from Cluny to Rome. She knew of no book which dealt specifically with the route but told me a story of one of the early abbots who, feeling death was near, asked his monks to carry him to Rome so that he could die there. On the way he became so ill that the monks thought he would die on the road and being nearer Cluny than Rome, they hurried back with the dying abbot who then recovered and lived another few years in Cluny before keeping his appointment with death. The library was fascinating. Besides tomes of theology and Scripture, there were ancient volumes on mathematics, medicine, architecture, and comparative religion, besides some large fifteenth-century tomes on the Cluniac foundations in England.

The abbot's garden is now a public park and I spent the afternoon there under the shade of a tree in perfect peace until the silence was shattered by a group of forty schoolchildren who staggered in complaining loudly about blisters. They were on a sponsored walk and had just covered the first 24 kilometres. They had my sympathy as they hobbled about in their stockinged feet and made for the nearest water tap. Two of the children were leading a blind boy by the hand. He had walked with them and was one of the few who did not limp. After the children came two cars. The teachers had arrived with the food. For half an hour there was peace, until their meal was over and the youngsters began playing football. I envied them their speed of recovery. The teachers still looked exhausted from the car ride.

At 5 p. m. I left Cluny and took the D. 134, a very minor road towards Mâcon. It was a steep climb in the evening heat. At a small village called Igy, I called in at a cafe, which was full of revellers who had been celebrating July 14 with a fête in the village square outside the church. They were full of *liberté, égalité et fraternité,* and plied me with drink and questions. Where had I come from, whither, why, and where was my kilt? Was I walking because I was a Scot and did not like spending money? The question left them hysterical with laughter. But why did I not try *autostop,* which was quicker, more comfortable and cheaper? Alcoholic tears of laughter were running down their cheeks by this time. I told them that I preferred walking. 'But *monsieur* is not young,' said one woman, 'you must be about thirty. . . .' Vanity has its uses! I left the cafe with a light step, feeling twenty years younger.

Next day I reached Mâcon and crossed the Saône. It was a very flat stretch of road without shade, shops or restaurants. I called in at a farmhouse for water and a wash under the pump. The farmer had been in Scotland during the war, where he was stationed near Coatbridge and Wishaw, the heart of industrial Lanarkshire. He considered both towns '*trés beaux*'. *Toujours la politesse!*

It may have been two days of monotonous walking which made me long for company at this stage of the journey and I looked forward to Grenoble, where I was to spend a few days with friends and meet Colin Douglas, who would then accompany me across the Alps to the sea. At Villar-les-Dombes I found a public campsite late in the evening where the attendant refused to charge me anything because I was a real walker; a kind gesture, but I paid for it in another way. The campsite was infested with screaming children and I spent a restless night there until 4 a. m. Then followed three hours excellent walking in the cool of the morning. My route was through a succession of meres covered in delicate mist, the silence broken only by the cry of wildfowl.

In the evening I reached Chavanoz, south of the Rhône and while I was buying food for supper the rain began. I asked the shopkeeper if she could recommend a *pension*, or a place to camp for the night. 'Try *Monsieur le Curé*,' she said, 'he's a good man and will certainly give you a room.' So I made an exception to my rule about avoiding presbyteries and had a most interesting evening. *Monsieur le Curé* was a tough, cheerful-looking man in his thirties. He answered the door himself and gave me a room for the night. During the fierce thunderstorm later that evening, we sat over a bottle of wine in his study, which was lined with maps and photographs of archaeological digs. On the table were some of his finds. He was an amateur archaeologist, had gathered a group of youngsters around him who shared his interest and they had discovered a number of pre-Roman, Celtic settlements in the area. In rapid French he gave me a potted history of the migrations of some of the Celtic peoples, a walking race. Then he told me the sad story of the Catholic Church in this part of France. A few years ago there were eleven priests in the area; today there are only three. One of the three had fourteen parishes to cover. The people still want to marry and be buried in the Church, but only 4 per cent are regular church-goers.

South of Chavanoz the walking was more interesting, over hills and through woodland. I felt sorry for the motorists I passed, baking in their little boxes, looking exhausted and apparently bored, while I was enjoying walking. I was feeling at one with myself, with the road, with the countryside and walking with the frame rucksack which tilted my body slightly forward, I felt at one as well with those pre-Celtic ancestors of ours who had also moved along with their arms swinging slightly in front of their legs.

The sky grew heavy again that evening and I called at a farmhouse where three young boys were playing. They ran in to summon their father, who greeted me with a smile, apologized for the muddiness of his courtyard and said I was welcome to pitch a tent anywhere. He explained that he had just bought this derelict property, was in the process of gutting the farmhouse and hoped to be living in it in a year's time. I had just set up my tent when the youngest of the boys came out and asked: 'Would *monsieur* care to have an *apéritif?*' I followed him into the broken-down building, whose sole furniture was a table and two benches and we had our *Pastis* out of huge mugs. As the rain began, I left them hurriedly in order to fasten up my tent, just before the storm broke. In the height of the storm the same youngster returned: 'Would *monsieur* care to join us for supper?' I had just finished my own supper, but joined them later for coffee. We talked about house prices, inflation, education and then the boys escorted me across the mud to my tent with torches and invited me to join them for breakfast in the morning. The family reminded me of Harry and Cathy Campbell in their readiness to welcome the stranger and share what they had.

Next day I had my first view of the mountains in the

110

distance, and seeing them was like meeting old friends. I stopped to gaze at them and wanted to give them the Glasgow greeting, 'Hullorer' (Hello there), but mountains are like grave and elderly friends, touchy about over-familiarity. I stand in awe of mountains and would never affront their dignity. It would be like greeting an elderly cardinal with 'Hullorer, Charlie'. If you treat mountains with respect they will share their secrets with you, but if you take liberties, they can brush you aside to your death. I was on mountains with a group of ten students one day in winter a few years ago, before I had learned to respect them. We were in a hurry to descend because it was snowing hard and visibility was worsening. One of the party slipped and I tried to catch her, lost my footing and we both fell 90 metres. She was very fortunate not to have been killed as she hit a rock and suffered a deep gash on the forehead. I landed in soft snow about 30 metres below and was only slightly scraped. It took the remainder of the party an hour to reach us. They were led by a French student, Madeleine Templier, an experienced climber. For three hours we waited in the bitter cold while someone went for a search party and stretcher for the injured girl. So when I saw the mountains in the distance I refrained from 'Hullorer' and touched my forelock instead

On the hills above Voiron I could see the great valley of the Isère river enclosed by its steep, tree-covered hills. There were many reminders of World War II in the villages I passed through, little plaques commemorating members of the *Maquis* killed in action or shot by the German occupants, other plaques celebrating their day of liberation by British troops. Near Voiron a large plaque recalled the death by torture of many innocent people in May 1944, 'in defiance of all human rights'.

On Sunday morning, July 20, I walked down the valley of the Isère, flanked by steep hills, the white stone glittering in the sunlight. At Mass in a church just south of Voreppe I fell asleep during the sermon and woke half an hour later for the offertory. At 2 p. m. I was in Grenoble, so fascinated by the beauty of the city with its background of snow-covered peaks that I kept stopping to look, obstructing passers-by with

111

the bulky rucksack. Madeleine Templier's family had kindly offered to put me up for a few days and I had arranged to meet Madeleine outside the main post office in Grenoble at 3 p. m.

I sat waiting in the little square near the post office, brewed a cup of coffee and then stretched out on a bench in the hot sun in a daze, not very sure whether I really had been on the road for over four weeks, had covered half the distance to Rome and was now in Grenoble. I lifted my boots from the ground beside the bench. The thick vibram soles with which I left Weybridge were now without tread and there was little rubber left. My arms and legs were mahogany-coloured and the soles and heels of my feet were extremely hard.

But the more important change was within me. I felt a great sense of peace, the peace of at-oneness, and I prayed that I would never lose it but grow in it. In this peace I felt I was seeing more, hearing more, living more fully and I could better understand Paul's prayer for the Ephesians,

> Out of his infinite glory may he give you the power through his Spirit for your hidden self to grow strong, so that Christ may live in your hearts through faith, and then, planted in love and built on love, you will with all the saints have strength to grasp the breadth and length, the height and the depth of his love; until knowing the love of Christ which is beyond all knowledge, you are filled with the utter fullness of God.

8

Mountain Welcome

Madeleine Templier met me at the post office and drove me to her parents' home on the Route de Chambery a few kilometres north-east of Grenoble. It was a beautiful house set on a hillside, its verandah and wide windows looking out across the valley to the snow-covered alpine peaks.

Madeleine had spent 1968–69 in Glasgow as an assistant teacher, part of her degree course in English from Grenoble University. Besides teaching and attending courses at Glasgow University, she also acquired an extensive knowledge of the Scottish mountains in climbing and skiing, had a large circle of Scottish friends and became fascinated by the Glasgow dialect, the like of which she had never heard from her Grenoble professors. She always carried a small notebook which was whipped out whenever she heard a new word or expression. The students assured her that if she wanted to hear 'pure Glesca' she must go to Barrowland, Glasgow's open market, where on any Sunday afternoon 'Glesca' can be heard at its loudest and most primitive. She went, but she could not write fast enough to capture this new and fascinating language, nor could her notebook record the inflections and rhythm of Barrowland's hucksters, so she returned with a tape recorder and based her degree dissertation on a forty-minute tape-recording. When she returned to Grenoble, her professors were delighted at her scientific study, which illustrated the originality, rich imagery, rhythm and syllabic economy of 'Glesca', but they were horrified at the accent she had acquired in her researches and warned her that she must revert to BBC English for examination purposes. I told her that she should place two very hot potatoes in her mouth

113

and keep on repeating, 'Would you care to fly by Imperial Airways?' She has now lapsed back into BBC but can still rise to rhythmic, imaginative and syllabically economic 'Glesca' with a little encouragement.

Monsieur Templier, her father, is an experienced alpinist. In his retirement from business he has now taken up a new alpine sport, parachuting from a plane onto alpine snows. He was very interested in the details of my walk, studied maps with me, suggested possible routes through the Alps, spent hours phoning friends of his along the route to arrange camping places and gave me letters of introduction to other friends.

I had my first bath that night for over five weeks, and although I knew hot water was not good for my heels and would soften them, I took the risk and was quite prepared to trade present pleasure for future pain. My bedroom window looked out on the mountains and I sat for a long time gazing at their shadowy forms in the night sky.

The Monday morning feeling was good on this occasion and I felt fully awake as dawn was breaking. I watched the changing colours on the mountains from the verandah upstairs, and after re-reading the pile of letters which I had collected the night before I began to answer them. The Templiers had suggested sightseeing tours for the next three days, but I told them that I would be very happy to sit on the verandah with an occasional visit to Grenoble.

Madeleine and a teacher friend of hers took me into Grenoble later in the morning to do some shopping and visit the Jesuit house there. We found a cobbler, who renewed the vibram soles and heels of my boots. He presented me with the old ones, which were paper-thin at the ball of the foot. An elderly priest answered the door at the Jesuit residence, where I wanted to say Mass later in the day. He blinked at the three of us and blinked more rapidly still when I introduced myself as a fellow Jesuit. He then asked whether *mon père* would care to stay for lunch, or would prefer to dine with *les desmoiselles*. As I had already arranged to go with the *desmoiselles* to *le Milk Bar*, I declined his invitation, but asked if I might come two days later with Colin Douglas, a Church of Scotland minister. The old priest looked more puzzled than ever, but said we would be welcome. I cannot now remember the order of the evening meal which Madame Templier gave us on our return, but there seemed to be an endless succession of courses and flagons of red wine. Conversation was easy because when I got lost in a sentence, Madeleine would come to the rescue, let me speak in English and give a simultaneous translation.

I spent most of the following day sitting writing. By evening both my legs, especially the ankles, were swollen and felt very tight. They were not painful, but the slight discomfort worried me. This tightness remained until I began walking again.

Early on the Wednesday morning I went into Grenoble to meet Colin arriving on the night train from Paris. He looked pale and tired, but rejected my suggestion that he should spend the rest of the day sleeping to recover his strength before beginning the Alps on Thursday. We called in at the Jesuit house for lunch and had an hilarious meal as Colin dug deep into his memory to find the *mot juste* in answer to the questions fired at him on the difference between Anglicans and Presbyterians, ministers and elders. The community referred to me as *mon père*, were uncertain how they should address Colin and eventually settled for *père pasteur*. One member of the community was a very talkative and outspoken man. He began to question me about the walk, why I was doing it and where I had started from. The elderly priest whom I had met two days before was showing great interest. Eventually, my interrogator moved into his final question and the elderly priest's blinks became even more rapid. 'Is it true, *mon père*, that you are walking to Rome with two *desmoiselles?*' '*Malheureusement, non,*' I replied. The elderly priest smiled and stopped blinking. That evening Madame Templier produced an even longer meal with enough food to see us through the Alps.

On Thursday morning Madeleine drove Colin and myself to the post office at Grenoble so that I could continue the walk from the point at which I had stopped and at 6.30 a. m. Colin and I were walking towards the mountains.

My legs were still feeling tight and Colin's knees felt weak,

Grenoble to La Spezia

but we kept up a brisk pace and just after midday, having done most of the distance we intended for that first day, we stopped in a shady field for four hours where Colin made up some of his lost sleep. In the evening we walked for an hour and reached our camping place for the night, a field belonging to a carpenter friend of Monsieur Templier. There was a restaurant nearby, where we were both feeling slightly disappointed with the meal of salad, ham and peaches when the waitress reappeared and we realised we had only had the hors d'oeuvres. When we returned to our camping place in the dark, the carpenter met us and invited us to his house for coffee and liqueurs. Colin was beginning to appreciate what Protestantism had lost by neglecting the Catholic tradition of pilgrimage!

For the route across the Alps I had planned on roughly 22 kilometres each day instead of the usual 32. The first two days of walking were along the main road, the N. 85 to Vizille and then along the N. 91 through the Gorge de la Romanche, a deep valley formed by the river which cuts its way through the hills. It was a disappointing route at first with heavy traffic on the roads, which made conversation difficult, and we trudged along in single file past factories and rock quarries. When I was studying the map of the Grenoble Gap a few months earlier, I had a curious dream in which I walked along a road between beautiful mountain peaks, but the road itself was a road in industrial Lanarkshire, lined with ugly factories. The reality was not quite as ugly as the dream and the mountain peaks in the distance promised better things to come.

On our second day we came to Le Bourg d'Oisans, a most beautiful town and a popular centre for mountain climbers and skiers. We camped in a field belonging to more friends of the Templiers, a magnificent spot about 2 kilometres from the town and near to the road which zig-zags its way up to the famous ski resort of Huez. We set up our tents in the shade of tall poplars as the sun was still very warm, but when evening came, the air cooled rapidly and I wore a thick pullover for the first time since leaving Weybridge. On our departure from Grenoble, the Templiers had presented us with a half-bottle of champagne to celebrate our arrival when we reached Le Bourg d'Oisans, so we cooled it in a stream and drank to all our absent friends. For supper I had bought a bottle of Les Vieux Papes to try out on Colin.

For the next two days we had planned a route along one of the Sentiers de Grande Randonnée, a mountain track which would take us up over the Col de Saronne, to a village called Besse, where we would camp for the night. The following day, still following the *sentier*, we would cross the Plateau d'en Paris and spend that night in the Templier chalet at Ventelon, just above La Grave. Madeleine had arranged to meet us on the Saturday morning at Le Bourg d'Oisans and collect our rucksacks, which she would then take by car to Besse. On Sunday morning, the Templiers would join us in Besse for Mass, then take our rucksacks on to friends of theirs in Monetier-les-Bains, a town 23 kilometres along our route beyond Ventelon. As the chalet at Ventelon had all mod. cons., we could travel light with a minimum of equipment for the next three days.

As Colin was under no self-imposed obligation to walk all the way, I suggested that he should wait behind at our camping place for Madeleine on the Saturday morning while I climbed up to Huez, about 1,200 metres above us, and he could come up later by car. It was bitterly cold when I left the camp at 6.30 a. m. Without the weight on my back, I felt I was walking with springs on my feet and I was still cold when I reached the winding road to Huez. To improve my circulation and save time I started cutting the bends in the road and proceeded in a direct line up the hill. The slope grew steeper. I continued obstinately, clambering over rocks and catching hold of branches until I found myself at one point unable to find a hand or foothold in front and afraid of slipping if I tried to move back. The longer I hesitated, the more I realized my predicament and my knees began shaking. There were some trees ahead just out of reach and the route looked safe. I took a deep breath, thanked God for the new vibram soles and lunged forward to grab the nearest branch. As I held it, I vowed never to take short cuts either up or down steep hills again. (Ten days later I took another short cut, which frightened me even more, but it was on flat ground.) As soon as I reached the main road again I stayed on it and had two hours excellent walking, now looking north, now south as the road twisted its way out of the valley. I was in Huez having breakfast by the roadside when Madeleine and Colin arrived by car.

There were many occasions in the course of the walk when I wished I could believe in reincarnation; the walk along these alpine paths was one of them. I would like to live in the mountains and spend my days climbing and skiing, parachute-jumping and gliding but I have not much time left for any of these activities. I once heard heaven described as a state where everything in us is going full throttle, and I hope that is a true description.

Colin and I started on our way along the *sentier* which follows the roaring Saronne. The gorge was bordered with wild flowers and widened as we climbed up to the Col de Barolles (2,000 metres). To the south-west we could see La Meije (4,000 metres) and near it the fierce-looking ridges of Le Rateau. The air was cool in the bright sun at the summit of the Col but, as we descended into the valley on the far side, the afternoon heat became intense. We passed a tiny village on the hillside where a group of peasant women were cutting hay with hand sickles along the steep gradients where no machine could reach. The village streets were narrow, rutted farm tracks running between the houses, so built that they seemed to defy all the laws of gravity. The roofs made only occasional contact with the walls, which bulged alarmingly. Even this tiny and remote village had its cafe and we rested there until Madeleine appeared and showed us the way to Besse, a slightly larger village, built on an even steeper hillside. We walked the length of it and a kilometre beyond before we could find a patch of ground with a slope gentle enough to allow us to pitch our tents.

The village had a narrow metalled road running through it, adequate for its normal traffic of mule carts, but on this Saturday the road was filled with Fiats, Renaults and some expensive-looking Mercedes. All its inhabitants were standing outside the church in a state of great excitement. A local girl

119

was marrying a man from Páris. The young girls were no doubt envying the lucky bride, who was going to spend the rest of her life in the big city, and I wondered if the bride would one day envy her envying friends when she remembered the beauty of their home in the mountains.

We both had an uncomfortable evening, because of insects, close relatives of the sabre-toothed midge, and the slope on which we had pitched our tents. A simple north-south slope is manageable, but when the ground also slopes east-west it is difficult to lie still.

On Sunday morning the Templier family came over to meet us and I said Mass in the little village church, the most physically uncomfortable Mass I have ever celebrated. On the previous evening the wedding guests had been treated to a slide show in the church illustrating the history of Besse through the ages. The screen had been hung at an angle over the altar and had not been removed. It was a large screen held in position by a complicated system of rigging, and I did not dare try to remove it, so I celebrated Mass stooped at an angle corresponding to the slope of the screen.

After Mass and our final farewell to the Templier family, Colin and I set out on our climb over the Plateau d'en Paris to Ventelon, a route which M. Templier had told us was the most beautiful stretch of walking in the whole area. We were not disappointed. For most of the day we were on a plateau with La Meije and Le Rateau closer to us now to the southwest. On our ascent we could hear the *marmottes*, little bearlike alpine animals, who spend the winter hibernating and the summer eating and playing on the mountains. I never cease to wonder at the stupidity of a thesis we were given in philosophy which stated, *Bruta intellectu carent* – (Animals are without intelligence).

The descent from the plateau towards Ventelon was gradual and we ran down most of it in order to reach the village before the shops closed. At 6 p. m. we were in Ventelon but the shops were already closed and we were told we could find food in La Grave, a town lower down the valley. The Templier chalet was perched high on the hill. Almost the whole of one side was window which looked south onto the

snow-covered slopes of La Meije, whose colours changed from
a delicate pink to lilac and then to a deep purple as the sun
went down. Colin was suffering from slight sunburn and
fatigue and offered to prepare the supper while I went down
to La Grave where I found a supermarket and bought a large
supper and a bottle of wine. Near the supermarket was a
most beautiful twelfth-century church. Dusk was falling and
the little church was illuminated by coloured candles of
varying shapes.

We had a very Scots supper of soup, potatoes, a variety of
other vegetables, cold ham and fruit salad, but acknowledged
the place with a bottle of wine. We sat facing out in the same
direction and watched night fall over the mountains.

I did not feel like bed and sat on the table after Colin
had retired. The slopes of La Meije seemed luminous in the
darkness. I sat recalling the last two days, the views we had
enjoyed, the people we had met, our conversations. I had
climbed many mountains in Scotland with Colin, almost
always with a group of students. Non-climbers would ask us,
'What's the point of climbing up mountains and then
climbing down again?' There was no point in trying to
convince them by argument, but if we could persuade them
to come with us, most of them stopped asking silly questions
and became hill-walking addicts.

Mountains are awe-inspiring, like sacraments of God's
presence. After a day in their presence, something of their
stillness seeps into the soul. Worries and anxieties which once
seemed so important fade into perspective, the perspective of
our tininess and insignificance in the face of the mystery of
the universe. As I looked out at La Meije that evening my
small-mindedness, preoccupations and irritability seemed so
ridiculous when I looked on those peaks, beautiful and threatening. There they stood, massive, majestic, millions of years
old, and we, ant-like creatures with our tiny life-span, crawl
halfway up them and feel proud of our achievement. Yet
somehow because we can appreciate their grandeur we
become at one with them, rejoice that they are there and ask
them to bless the Lord as the psalmist did. But St Paul brings
the mountains even nearer and helps us to feel at one with

them when he writes to the Colossians, 'In Christ all created things have their being, heavenly and earthly, all things were created through him and for him.' What is our Christian faith about? It is acknowledging, relishing, celebrating the truth that all the mystery of our existence can find its meaning in the Word that was made flesh, who shared our lives and our death, so that in death we might live. Christ said, 'This is my body, given for you,' as he gave the bread to his disciples. Our existence is a gift of a loving God and, no matter how dark or however tragic it may be for us, it is never hopeless because God has come down into our darkness and death and is risen again. I prayed for faith to see God in all creation and all creation in him. Then another voice began in me.

'You are escaping into vague and woolly thoughts, the result of pleasant physical tiredness, a good supper and a bottle of wine, but those thoughts are unreal. Even your vision of the mountains is unreal. They are seductive, cruel and savage. They cast a spell on men, draw them on and, when they are near the summit, let loose their avalanches on them and hurl them down their icy flanks to their death. A sign of God's presence! A splendid sign of his presence, because he, too, seduces men and women and draws them to throw their lives away, to renounce father, mother, brother, sister, possessions, independence, in order to serve him. Off they go, full of hope and expectation to climb the mountain of God, entering the gates of the seminary or noviciate. There they meet "safe" guides who show them how to scale the heights by observing "the rule", putting in the statutory time in "spiritual duties", attending their three meals a day punctually and with due religious decorum and obeying their religious superiors as if they were Christ himself. And in your name, and out of love for you, they keep their rule, not because it is easy or pleasant, but because they have faith in you. So they live in arid isolation awaiting your coming, more dead than alive. If they complain that their life seems to them, in their more honest moments, to be a waste of time, then they are told that they must pray more and beg for faith.'

As I argued in prayer I saw the unfairness of my

complaints. God is not to be blamed for our religious stupid-
ities, but we are to be blamed if we do not learn from them.
He is the God of love who gives us freedom. Religious rules
and regulations are only justified in so far as they help us to
respond to his love and grow in his freedom. If they are
observed in any other way, they can destroy us.

I experienced a strange restlessness as I looked out at La
Meije. The sight stilled me, but the very stillness made me
afraid of losing what I was experiencing. I was catching
glimpses through the prison bars of my own mind and wanted
to be set free. I prayed to God to break down the barriers of
my certainty, security, respectability, my systems, rules and
categories which keep me safe, so that I could find him outside
the camp, where the helpless and the hapless live without
any evidence of his presence. I wanted to be a pilgrim all my
life long, a wanderer, uncertain of my destination, certain
only that God is faithful and that if I search for him, he will
find me.

We left the chalet at Ventelon at nine the following
morning, Monday, July 28, and cut down the steep hill to
meet the main N. 91 in the valley below, climbing again over
a 10–kilometre stretch to the Col du Lautaret. Although the
sun was very hot, the walking was easy because we were still
free of our rucksacks until we reached Monetier-les-Bains and
found the hotel where the Templiers had left them. The sky
grew heavy as we approached the town and the rain began
as we sat in a cafe which quickly filled with climbers and
hikers, including a group of children with some spastics
among them.

We set off in the rain after waiting an hour. We were both
suffering from sore feet and Colin was beginning to experience
some of the more penitential aspects of pilgrimage, but he
had been brought up in one of these 'run-and-cold-shower-
before-breakfast' schools whose motto was *Sparta natus es, hanc
exorna* (Add lustre to your native Sparta), a motto which I
repeated to him frequently before we reached the sea. It was
still raining when we reached Villeneuve where we camped
in a field next to a *colonie de vacances* for a hundred children
from Marseilles, whose French we could not understand and

who found our French, which they mimicked, a source of endless laughter.

Briançon looked very attractive from the distance, but when we reached the town it was so jammed with traffic and tourists that we did not stop for sightseeing. The only pleasure on the road out of Briançon with cars passing every few seconds was the thought that each step was taking us further away from the crowds and the noise, but the steps were tiring and we were both very weary when we reached La Roche de Rame where we camped for the night and decided to take things easy next day. Even the Spartans took occasional rest.

A few kilometres beyond La Roche de Rame we turned off the main N. 94 and took the N. 202 into Guillestre where we arrived at midday and rested before beginning the climb over the Col de Vars. To celebrate our arrival and our day of rest, we stopped at a restaurant on a hill above the town, sat in its shaded garden and ordered a carafe of wine. An hour later we ordered a sandwich lunch and were each given a large loaf filled with butter and very salty salami. This naturally called for another carafe of wine. After three hours rest in the shaded garden we felt ready to tackle the Col de Vars. Half an hour later, both parched with thirst, exhausted by the intense heat and the steep climb, we rested for another hour. Hilaire Belloc must have had an extraordinary constitution when he did his walk to Rome. His *Path to Rome* is peppered with descriptions of the quantity and quality of the wine he drank on his way, fuel for the journey. I found wine dehydrating and enervating.

The climb up to the Col was steep at first, then more gradual, but it seemed an endless road. At Vars we found a genial hotel proprietor who allowed us to camp in the garden at the back of the hotel provided we could be away by 8 a. m. when his guests would breakfast there. We had a supper dictated by our thirst, of shandy, tomatoes, fruit and milk and looked out over the mountains with a view of Mont Pelvoux in the distance. It was already dark by the time we had eaten.

The next day was Thursday, July 31, feast day of St Ignatius, founder of the Jesuits who led the Counter-Reformation.

Four hundred years later I was celebrating his feast in the company of Colin, a Presbyterian minister. We had agreed to spend the first hour's walking of each day in silence and I thought about Ignatius as he reveals himself in the *Spiritual Exercises*, a very different character from 'the soldier saint' of some popular writing which makes him out to be some kind of papal Napoleon. His 'Contemplation to Obtain Love' with which he ends the *Spiritual Exercises*, begins with a typical Ignatian observation, 'Love ought to manifest itself in deeds rather than in words,' followed by

Love consists in a mutual sharing of goods, e.g. the lover gives and shares with the beloved what he possesses, or something of that which he has or is able to give, and vice versa, the beloved shares with the lover. Hence, if one has knowledge, he shares it with the one who does not possess it, and so also if one has honours or riches. Thus one always gives to the other.

The exercise that follows consists in trying to see every moment of existence in the light of this truth, that in everything God is communicating himself to me what he possesses, his very self.

Reflect how God dwells in creatures, in the elements giving them existence, in the plants giving them life, in the animals conferring on them sensation, in man bestowing understanding. So he dwells in me and gives me being, life, sensation, intelligence. Reflecting on this truth I will make this offering of myself, 'Take, Lord, and receive all my liberty, my memory, my understanding and my entire will, all that I have and possess. You have given all to me, to you Lord, I return it. All is yours, dispose of it wholly according to your will. Give me your love and your grace, for this is sufficient for me.'

As we walked up to and over the Col de Vars I thought about this contemplation and gave Colin a potted history of the Jesuits. They are so often portrayed as a military religious order, men who have handed over their own will and intelligence to the will of their superior, their ultimate commander-

125

in-chief on earth being the Pope. They are thought of by those who do not know them as men for whom the end justifies the means, and the end is the greater glory of the Roman Catholic Church, whose glory is strength in political, financial and ecclesiastical power. Ignatius is pictured as a clerical Napoleon who trained his shock troops to put obedience above every other virtue.

In fact, obedience was the last vow which he and his companions took, and the reason they took it was that they wanted to have some kind of bond which would hold them together as friends in the Lord when their work scattered them throughout the world. Ignatius was a mystic who could weep at the sight of a flower. 'Consider,' he writes in that same contemplation, 'how God works and labours for me in all creatures on the face of the earth; that is, he conducts himself as one who labours. Thus in the heavens, the elements, the plants, the fruits, the cattle etc., he gives being, conserves them, confers life and sensation. Then I will reflect upon myself and consider, according to all reason and justice, what I ought to offer the Divine Majesty, that is, all I possess and myself with it.'

Ignatius spent the latter part of his life in translating these ideals of the Exercises into detailed application, administering and organizing the body of men who had joined him after making the Exercises (they numbered a thousand at his death), and in writing the Jesuit Constitutions. The spirit which informed these Constitutions was the spirit of the 'Contemplation to Attain Love'. As with any other body, it is the spirit which gives life: the letter kills. I thought of my own life as a Jesuit. I owe so much to this Society of Jesus that I feel mean in making any criticism of it in writing. But the object of our existence is not the greater comfort and complacency of our fellow members, it is the pursuit of an ideal which binds us together, namely, the greater glory of God. We totter and stagger often in our search and take wrong routes, but that is better than sitting still. Ignatius, at one time in his life, used to sign himself as 'the pilgrim'. He was a searcher, always looking for the greater glory of God. One of the principles for choosing work which he gives in the

Constitutions is 'the more universal the good is, the more it is divine'. His spirit of search characterized the early Jesuits who travelled all over the world and were so inventive and imaginative. When they became well-known and established they reflected the transformation from a pilgrim Church to a parade-ground Church.

As a body of men in England, after the pioneering days of Campion and Persons there and of Ogilvie in Scotland, we tended to settle down, with a few notable exceptions, and to be content to work within the Roman Catholic body. We have been more interested in sailing Catholic lagoons than the seas of God's goodness, sailing very correctly, sometimes very skilfully, navigating not by the stars but by the rules of hierarchical right order. In the noviciate we were taught that virtue consists in 'doing ordinary things extraordinarily well' and that we should pray for a life 'hidden with Christ in God'. Teaching small boys the elements of Latin and Greek extraordinarily well in a Jesuit college hidden away in the country could therefore be seen as an expression of Ignatius' ideals in the Exercises. That there can be great virtue in such an occupation I do not deny, but such an interpretation tends to blind us to other important truths and so produces men whose main preoccupation in life may become new methods of teaching the use of the Latin ablative absolute or the disciplinary details of a well-ordered school, with a corresponding horror of anything which might upset the even tenor of their ways.

Suggestions that we should look beyond the school walls at the spiritually starved in urban jungles, that we should ask whether the provision of fee-paying schools for the comparatively wealthy is really the most important work we could be doing, have been looked upon as signs of spiritual restlessness, of refusal to remain 'hidden with Christ in God' and to do ordinary things extraordinarily well. In the Catholic Church in Britain the same criticism could be made of its priests and Religious, namely that they are more content to work strictly within the fold than to attempt a wider apostolate. So much of our work within the Catholic Church is directed to keeping the institution going that it ceases to be catholic in its literal sense, i.e. universal. My own experience of the former pupils of Catholic schools indicates the failure of our option for maintenance rather than mission. The maintenance does not seem to maintain and perhaps we have to learn that faith is not for keeping, but for spreading; that when we direct all our energies to preserving it, we stifle it. Christ's words, 'Unless you lose your life you cannot find it,' are applicable to the Church as a body as well as to its individual members, and until it becomes a Church with a sense of mission to all men, it cannot grow.

I was walking up this hill over the *col* with Colin, Catholic priest and Protestant minister, a partnership which many people found surprising: the only surprising thing about it being that it should be considered surprising. We were both trying to serve the one God whom we both believed had spoken his word in Christ, in whom we both live and move and have our being. Yet we have our separate schools, our separate churches, separate preoccupations in keeping our respective institutions going, convinced that we are right and that those who disagree with us are wrong. We forget in our zealous efforts that the God we serve is the 'wholly Other', whose thoughts are not our thoughts and whose ways are not our ways. He can be approached only in a spirit of humility, which acknowledges our own and our Church's sinfulness and ignorance, so that something of his gentleness, magnanimity and love can take hold of our being and impel us to leap over the ecclesiastical barricades which separate us and so share together in the life of his poor.

'He put aside his divinity and became a slave for love of us,' St Paul tells the Philippians. As love is a mutual interchange, we ought to put aside our privileged economic, social and, perhaps above all, theological security which can mislead us into thinking that we have found the answers instead of realizing that we have to search for them and that a condition of our finding them is the love and unity that exist between Christians. 'Love', as Ignatius says, 'is shown in deeds rather than in words.' Ecumenism, working for the unity of Christians, is not an optional extra for the more fanatical: it lies at the heart of the gospel, and if we are not working for it, as distinct from making ecumenical noises from the bottom of our episcopal, priestly, religious hearts, then we are betraying Christ, no matter how extraordinarily well we are doing our ordinary jobs in our own sacristy or vestry. When Christians do work together 'to bring the good news to the poor, to proclaim liberty to captives and to give the blind new sight, to set the down-trodden free', then they experience the joy and peace of Christ and realize that theology is his servant, not his master.

'Disastrous and sentimental oversimplification'; I can hear the condemnations of some theologians and churchmen. I am writing about a walk and recording thoughts and impressions, not attempting a theological treatise and I can only answer, 'It is not half as disastrous as the over-conceptualization and rationalizing which has dessicated the Good News, making it unintelligible to the majority and a burden to many of the tiny minority who still adhere to it.'

That evening we reached St Paul, a beautiful village nestling between the mountain peaks. We celebrated St Ignatius with dinner in the hotel, our last meal in France, and camped afterwards in the hotel grounds.

It was still dark at 4 a. m. when I was woken by the cold. By five we were on the road, walking quickly to get the circulation going and to cover as much distance as possible before the heat began, usually around nine. After an hour's walking we joined the N. 100 and began the long climb to the Col de Larche, our last *col* before the entry to Italy. Then it would be downhill to Rome.

9

Light in the Darkness

The frontier area of Italy is wild and sparsely populated with occasional clusters of houses on the hillsides, where life continues as it must have been for centuries, men scraping a living from their little patch of land with a few goats and a cow or two. I wished the hills could speak and tell us the tale of those who had tramped this way before us, our Celtic ancestors, invading armies and medieval pilgrims, the Roman legionaries returning home to *Roma Aeterna* after service in Britain or Gaul.

Although the countryside looks the same on both sides of the border, there is no mistaking that you have arrived in another country. We were met at the border by a cigarette-smoking Italian passport officer, his assistant spread out on a bench nearby taking his ease and shattering the silence of the hills with canned music from his transistor. Beyond the frontier was the Lago della Maddalena, where we had our first introduction to Italian holiday-makers. They were very obviously enjoying themselves with loud transistors and even noisier children swarming everywhere. In the evening we reached Bersezio, 10 kilometres inside the Italian border where we camped on a hill behind the village. There was one shop with a notice outside authorizing the sale of tobacco and salt. Behind the shop was the village fountain, set in the middle of a square with houses on all four sides, and there we washed. There were people around who neither stared nor asked questions, doing nothing to make us feel we were foreigners.

On our second day in Italy the air was still, the temperature oven-like, the mountains shrouded in heavy mist. Although

our route was a gradual descent I was feeling very lethargic
while my companion was full of energy, a credit to the Old
School. After 14 weary kilometres we stopped at a bar and
asked where was the nearest restaurant. 'Up there,' said the
barman, pointing to the village of Sambuco high up on the
mountainside, 'or 10 kilometres further on.' Hunger drove us
off our route and we struggled up the hill to the village. I
was worried at my own lethargy and my leg was beginning
to swell slightly, but I felt no pain. Two days later, when the
swelling subsided I saw that I had been bitten by some insect
and hoped the lethargy was caused by the bite.

At the top of the village we found *il ristorante* and had the
most enormous meal which included soup, *pasta*, a large
platter of beef with potatoes and salad, cheese, genuine ice
cream and coffee. The meal cost us £1 each. The restaurant
was a most homely place, so very different from British
restaurants where groups tend to speak in subdued voices in
case their neighbours should overhear. In Italy they seem to
want everyone to hear and children have to shout to make
themselves heard above the noise of their elders. I had little
Italian at this stage and could not catch much of the conversation, but it was obviously centred on two babies in the
company. As I walked through Italy I saw examples of this
Italian love of children many times every day. The smaller
the child, the more it becomes an object of attention and
reverence. Even in the churches which are so often cluttered
with statues, the *Bambino*, sometimes in a glass case and
dressed like a doll, occupies the place of honour. In her
political chaos and the inability of any party to draw the
country together, why do they not appoint a *bambino* as Prime
Minister and so unite the country?

As I was a few pages ahead of Colin in my Italian phrase-
book, I left him by a fountain and went in search of a camping
place. I stopped to look at the church, built on a rock promon-
tory. A woman appeared from the sacristy with a vase of
flowers and greeted me with a loud '*Buon giorno*'. '*Buon giorno*',
I replied, and then began on the more difficult task of asking
for a camping place in my inchoate Italian. She listened
patiently to my efforts, laughed, took me by the arm and led

me into the sacristy to meet Don Angelo, a visiting priest, who could speak neither English nor French and so we talked in a mixture of Latin and Italian. Don Angelo then took me to meet a friend of his, Don Luigi, chaplain to a group of factory workers from Alba who had a holiday home in Sambuco. We were immediately invited to camp in the garden of their house and found ourselves entertaining a group of seventy men, women and children as we tried to pitch our tents and converse with them in our primitive Italian. They soon scattered when a fierce thunderstorm broke, which lasted for two hours. When it was over, Don Luigi emerged from the house and invited us to use the showers, solemnly presenting both of us with a tin of Johnson's baby powder before we entered. We joined the workers for supper, our conversation limited to exclamations. When learning a new language I tell many lies because I say what I can for the practice, which is not always what I mean.

After supper we joined them all for Mass in the village church, the Sunday Mass being commonly celebrated on Saturday evening in Italy. It was our first introduction to Italians at prayer in church, where their behaviour is only slightly more subdued than in a *ristorante*. They certainly possess that quality which St Ignatius demanded in a General of the Society of Jesus, 'familiarity with God'! After Mass we were invited by Don Angelo to meet some of his friends for coffee and Benedictine. The group included a number of young and very vivacious women whom we later discovered were religious sisters on holiday from a slum area in Genoa where they worked. After the Benedictine we were offered *Il Whisky* which, according to the label on the bottle, came from Ealing and tasted as though it might well have done. That evening when I called in at the grocer's shop to buy goods for the next day, the shopkeeper refused to take any money, telling me that Don Angelo had already paid for anything I might buy.

After breakfast with the workers' families next morning, we had a long period of farewells and a final photograph in which I was given the honour of holding the smallest baby present in my arms. As we descended the steep path to the main road, the families stood waving to us until we were well out of sight. We walked free of the load of our rucksacks which Don Luigi had offered to take by car to Demonte, 20 kilometres along our route.

The kindness we had met with in Sambuco coloured all my future impressions of Italy and Italians. Later I was to meet Italians who thieved, swindled, pushed and jabbed or who came perilously near to running me down in their cars, but they were exceptions and nothing could spoil that first impression in Sambuco where we were given such a warm, spontaneous and unexpected welcome.

Colin and I reached Demonte in the early afternoon and sat in sweltering heat outside the church waiting for Don Luigi to arrive with our rucksacks. As we sat on the pavement a woman came out of a house nearby and asked us what we were doing. She reappeared a few moments later with two glasses of wine and an addressed postcard, which she asked me to post to her on my arrival in Rome.

In France when I inquired about a place to camp for the night I received many a lecture on French law and warnings of what the *gendarmerie* would do if they caught me camping in an unauthorized place. In Italy people seemed puzzled that I even bothered to ask and would point to the nearest piece of level ground and say, 'Why not camp there?' So we camped at the edge of a copse in the town itself and nobody seemed to mind. Later in the evening we attended Mass which included a long sermon by a missionary priest who was collecting money for an African mission. Although I could only catch snatches of the meaning, I enjoyed listening to the rhythmic and flowing language accompanied by magnificent gestures. The congregation, however, looked bored. After Mass on Sunday evening the shops were still open and doing a brisk trade.

For the next two days we followed the river Demonte along paths and lanes through farms and orchards, walking early in the morning and late in the afternoon because the heat during most of the day made walking an endurance test more than a pleasure. We were in no hurry as we had arranged to meet a Glasgow couple, Jim and Pauline Gallacher, in Chiusa on Tuesday, August 5, at 9 p. m. outside its main church. If they failed to turn up, our next rendezvous was to be at 5 p. m. on the steps of Genoa cathedral on Saturday, August 9.

Jim and Pauline had both been students at Glasgow University while I was there and they had first met at a student conference I had organized at Lochailort in 1968. I had celebrated their wedding just before leaving Glasgow in April 1975. Jim had been my first climbing companion and is the only person I know who can keep talking the whole way up and the whole way down a mountain: gales, snowstorms, near-vertical gradients notwithstanding. One day we climbed three munros in succession (mountains of over 950 metres) and on another day we climbed the five sisters of Kintail. Jim was still discussing the iniquities of our capitalist system at the end of both climbs. Pauline studied Fine Arts and struggled up many a mountain with us, but she is a more meditative walker, preferring to save her energy for the next step.

We reached Chiusa at midday on August 5, sampled its wine which was excellent, its ice cream which was better still, and then searched for a place to rest out of the sun. We had just set up our tents in a field when we heard the roll of distant thunder. To avoid a soaking, we took refuge with the local parish priest who received us with some suspicion at first, but ended by inviting us to supper. Conversation was difficult as Latin was our only common tongue, not the language for a party even when you can remember it. My Latin was rusty, Colin's eroded, and we were limited once again to making exclamations. It is hard to establish a chummy relationship on *bene, optime* and *mehercule!*

The storm raged outside during our supper, but abated about 8.30 p. m. when we took up watch outside the church and waited for the white Renault with a Glasgow registration. It was already dark and the rain had that quality which the Irish call 'soft', a light persistent drizzle which penetrates to the marrow and stiffens the joints. White Renaults are the most popular cars in Europe and most of them seemed to be passing through Chiusa that night, raising our hopes then dashing them. By 10 p. m. we abandoned hope of meeting.

Our next meeting place at Genoa cathedral was 140 kilometres away, which meant 35 kilometres for the next four days, not difficult in normal conditions, but too much for comfort in this August heat. We therefore decided to try night walking, starting this very evening. We checked our torches because the night was black and found that neither of them was working. Remembering Sparta, we stepped out into the night.

The drizzle in which we started turned to heavy rain and then we heard the thunder again, rolling up from the distance and exploding uncomfortably near us. We stopped at a cafe, still crowded although it was almost midnight, and had a cup of coffee. I envied the revellers as they finished off their drinks and went to their cars to drive home to a bed for the night.

The thunderstorm passed while we were in the cafe and the rain was soft again as we left. Our eyes soon became accustomed to the darkness and it was not difficult to follow the road. I began to enjoy the stillness of night walking, the heavy smell of the woods after the rain and the chorus of insects singing in the shadows. Colin was troubled with foot cramp, but he did Sparta proud, walking along with a most curious step, as though he were trying to shake the cramp out of his boots. We had grown so accustomed to the dark that I thought we could risk a short cut across farm tracks from Roccaforte to Vasco, which I reckoned would save us about 8 kilometres. It might have done had I not missed a turn near Casco which led us 5 kilometres out of our way. It was still dark when we reached the main road again and rested in the courtyard of the church in Mondovi. At Sambuco they had told us that we must not miss the famous church at Mondovi, but all that we saw at 5.30 a. m. was the outline of its magnificent dome.

Dawn brings hope and a sudden surge of energy to the night walker, but the energy is a short-term loan. We decided to stop at the first hotel/*pensione* we could find, rest for the day and recover energy for the next night's walk; a firm, resolute, unanimous decision which we could not implement for the next two hours as we trudged past the fields and the vineyards.

135

Near Lesegno we were directed to a hotel high on the hillside only to discover that its few rooms were already occupied. We sat in the hotel garden and ordered ice cream and lemonade for breakfast. It was a most extraordinary hotel garden with a miniature zoo for the entertainment of the guests, with cages of tropical birds, monkeys and owls. The only other occupant was a grey-haired man, oblivious of his surroundings, writing at a table piled high with notes. We reconsidered our firm decision made three hours before and I went off to look for a camping place for the day. In the course of the walk I began to notice that the occasions when I had difficulty in finding a place to camp and people seemed suspicious or indifferent were also the occasions when I was feeling very tired and irritated, and that my judgements, 'They are an unfriendly lot,' needed to be translated into, 'I am in an unfriendly mood'. But I had still not learned that lesson and returned to Colin with the news that the villagers were unfriendly and we would have to camp where we could without anyone's permission. The village school, closed for the summer holidays, was near the hotel and we pitched our tents in the grass playground. Colin managed to sleep but I lay in my tent, restless and bathed in sweat.

I took my writing-pad and returned to the restaurant where the grey-haired man was still at work on his notes. A group of children came in to buy ice cream, among them a ten-year-old French girl who was on a visit to her Italian cousins. She fired questions at me, was a born gossip, told me about her own and her cousins' family and that the grey-haired man was a German professor who spent his days writing notes in the garden. She then told me that I spoke French very well and wanted to know where I had learned it. I was riding the crest of this compliment, when a sleepy, dishevelled Colin appeared ready for his lunch. I greeted him. 'Is that your son?' asked my interrogator.

The hotel manager presented us with a glass of 'Irish Mist' at the end of lunch, which helped us to another firm decision to do no more night walking. We would walk as far as we could until Saturday morning, when Colin would then leave me and hitch, or take a train to keep his appointment with

Pauline and Jim on the steps of Genoa cathedral. When we collected water from the hotel later in the evening, the German professor was still at his notes.

On Thursday, August 7, we set out early and walked towards Ceva in silence for the first hour. After breakfasting on the pavement outside a Ceva grocer's shop, we were still walking in silence, which was not the silence of prayer but of a tiredness which left us with nothing to say to each other. A car hooted behind us, not an unusual occurrence on Italian roads, but this hooting was more persistent and irritating than usual. My irritation turned to delight when a white Renault with Glasgow registration pulled in ahead of us. Pauline and Jim had arrived, full of apologies for their delay.

It is hard to describe in words a meeting with friends. We use phrases like 'delighted to see you', 'glad to see you', but they are hopelessly inadequate. We do not usually say, 'You bring life back to me,' but that was what I felt. The sight of them brought back a flood of memories of themselves and of their friends, as though I were reliving them, and so rescued me from the narrow confines of my own tiredness. We sat in a field and celebrated our meeting. They handed me a pile of letters from Scotland. We consulted maps, and after choosing a spot 24 kilometres further on where we would meet that evening, Colin and I continued our walk, free of the weight of the rucksacks. I had given Jim and Pauline some hints on camping in Italy, telling them to find some suitable stretch of ground and then approach the nearest house to ask permission to use it. They did so that evening, finding a flat stretch of ground on a hillside overlooking a valley. The occupants of the nearby house were very friendly and allowed us to use their garden tap. We were enjoying our supper in the quiet of the evening when an irate woman appeared asking us what right we had to be camping there. Thoughtlessly, we pointed to the house at the end of the field, information which made the woman even more angry because she was the owner of the field. She was so disturbed at this high-handedness of her neighbours that she seemed to forget all about us and went off to launch her attack on them.

Colin and I started early the next morning, but by nine

the heat was already oppressive and the temperature rose as we approached Savona and the sea. The outskirts of Savona were drab and disappointing until we reached its promenade and I had my first sight of the Mediterranean, which did look blue and very peaceful. I felt for a moment as though the walk was over – just a short toddle along the sea front and then a drop down to Rome. In fact, the most strenuous part was still to come, but it is sometimes good that we have illusions and cannot see the future.

We had arranged to meet Jim and Pauline at Abisola Marina, a resort 5 kilometres east of Savona, at 2 p. m. and to spend the rest of the afternoon on the beach. The whole of Italy seemed to be on holiday on that stretch of the Riviera, the promenades lined with *bagni*, the sands hardly visible in the spaces between the umbrella sunshades. We struggled on to the beach after paying for entrance, changing cubicles and deck-chairs. The sand was so hot that it was uncomfortable to walk barefoot. I collapsed into a deck-chair and when I awoke two hours later the others were emerging as I entered the tepid water which had changed from blue to a murky grey. Swimming in that particular part of the Mediterranean is much more enervating than a 32–kilometre walk and it is no wonder that the holiday-makers need a long siesta in the afternoon. As we left the beach the crowds were returning to enjoy the last few hours of the sun. In Abisola we shopped for supper, dragging our Fine Arts student away from the art and ceramic shops to the more urgent business of food. We found a public campsite in the hills above the town and had a farewell supper for Colin who, having reached the sea and honoured Sparta was going on to Genoa next day by car.

Early on Saturday morning, Jim and Pauline drove me from the campsite back to the point in Abisola which I had reached on foot the day before and Pauline accompanied me for the first 8 kilometres of the 50–kilometre stretch to Genoa. There was no alternative route but the main road along this section of the walk. The Alps stretch down to the sea, so that inland walking cross-country would be an exhausting trek up and down hill. The *autostrada* runs parallel to the coast road to the north, a wonderful feat of engineering, mostly tunnel and viaduct. The coast road follows the shore, climbing over or tunnelling through the rocks which separate one bay from the next, each of which is a holiday resort. On the hills above the bays the wealthy have their villas and it took Pauline and me a long time to cover the first 8 kilometres as she stopped to admire the houses and give me some elementary lessons in architecture. When Jim and Colin came to collect her, I continued on my way over the hills and through the resorts, an enjoyable road until I reached Voltri and the industrial outskirts of Genoa. The city looks like a huge amphitheatre with the sea as its stage.

I met Colin on the steps of Genoa cathedral at 5 p. m., and a few minutes later Jim and Pauline arrived with friends of mine, Eileen and Augusto de Laurentiis and their son Raymondo. Eileen was from Glasgow and I had celebrated her wedding to Augusto in Glasgow a few years before. We arranged to meet them the following day for lunch and then said farewell to Colin, who had to leave Genoa by an early train the following morning and had booked in at a *pensione* near the station.

I was sorry to see him go. Not every friend is also a good walking companion but Colin combined both qualities. His enjoyment of the mountains increased my own and he had the great gift of seeing the funny side of a situation which, on my own, I would find merely irritating. His friendship too always reminds me that what we have in common across the denominations is far more important than what separates us. Walking alone and walking with a companion are two very different experiences and I was glad to have the experience of both. But if I were to do a long walk again, I would try to find someone to come with me, so I told Colin that I would let him know when I decided to walk to Jerusalem or to Compostella!

We camped that evening on a terraced hillside north of Voltri in landscape which looked very familiar because it was reminiscent of the background in so much Italian painting.

Genoa Cathedral is unlike any cathedral I had ever seen, built in black and white marble, very spacious within because it has no fixed chairs or benches, and lit by heavy and ornate chandeliers. We arrived late for the 10.30 Mass on Sunday morning. About 200 people were standing around a side altar in an otherwise empty cathedral and the choir were singing *Deo gratias* (Thanks be to God), which is the Latin response of the people to the priest's closing words at Mass, *Ite missa est* (Go, the Mass is finished). The side altar was thronged with clergy, wreathed in incense smoke, who then proceeded to the main altar followed by the Cardinal Archbishop of Genoa. It was then that I realised the *Deo gratias* was for the final vesting of the Cardinal and that Mass had yet to begin.

The Mass was a nostalgic occasion and brought back memories of Solemn High Mass in the days before the Second Vatican Council, the celebrants with their backs to the people, the slow and ordered movements across the sanctuary, the stylized gestures, clouds of incense, the precision and rhythm of the Latin prayers and, on this occasion, the beautiful polyphony of the choir. But I felt more like a spectator at a theatrical production and the congregation seemed more like sightseers than a people at prayer. It was very different from my experience at Vézelay and Taizé, where we all seemed to be taken up in the drama. In various countries there are groups of Roman Catholics who have formed themselves into a 'Latin Mass Society'. In so far as they are trying to preserve the Latin form of the Mass from extinction and find it helpful for their own life, they should be given every encouragement. Unfortunately, many of them go further than this and claim that any departure from Latin is a departure from orthodoxy. Their opposition to any change in the liturgy often includes opposition to any development in the Church's understanding of herself and so they weaken their case for preserving the Latin Mass.

The High Mass in Genoa ended with an announcement that a special indulgence (I had not enough Italian to hear how special) had been granted to those who had attended this Mass. I felt very angry at this announcement and was glad that Colin had not been present. When we told Jim Gallacher that he had just gained a special indulgence he launched into one of his anti-clerical rages, which abated only slightly when we had an ice cream in a nearby shop.

We drove up to the home of Eileen and Augusto high on the hill overlooking Genoa and could see why it has been described as 'Genoa the superb'. The flat was mercifully cool with its stone floor, high ceiling and large windows, and protected from the sun by venetian blinds. Eileen thoughtfully provided us with a meal more Scottish than Italian and we talked of Scotland, only moving to Italy when it was almost time for us to go.

As the weather was so hot, I wanted to try night walking again and suggested that we should look for a camping place somewhere near Chiavari, about 50 kilometres east of Genoa. We found an ideal place, a terraced orchard high on the hills and overlooking the bay of Rapallo. Later in the evening, Jim drove me back into Genoa so that I could continue walking without any 'wheeled thing' from the steps of Genoa cathedral. I felt very apprehensive that evening as we drove along the *autostrada* because the road seemed endless and I had to walk the whole distance, but by a different and more winding coast road, before breakfast next morning.

It was nearly midnight when we reached the centre of Genoa and made several attempts to find our way down one-way streets to the cathedral. I became impatient, told Jim to drop me in the main square, thought of Belloc's 'the essence of a vow is its literal meaning' and registered my disapproval by walking straight out of the city without returning the few hundred metres to pick up my trail at the cathedral. To the question, 'Did you really walk the whole way from Weybridge to Rome?' I have to answer, 'No, I crossed the channel by ferry and missed a few hundred metres in Genoa.'

Once clear of the city, the night walk was easy. The air was still and cool, the roads quiet. Apart from the chirruping of insects the only sound was the chugging of occasional motor boats in the bays below. The night sky was clear and I remembered Isaiah's words, 'He has stretched out the heavens like a cloth, spread them like a tent for men to dwell in.' I felt at home beneath them. As dawn was breaking I passed a church and a hundred metres further on two nuns passed me walking in the opposite direction. Thinking that they might be on their way to Mass in the church, I turned to follow. When they heard my steps following in the morning stillness, they quickened their pace and entered the church at a canter. When I entered there was no sign of them. I waited for ten minutes before taking to the road again and had a picture of the parish priest entering his sacristy to prepare for Mass, opening the vestment cupboard and finding two nuns closeted inside.

On the hill above the bay of Rapallo I passed a villa bearing the plaque, 'Max Beerbohm lived here'. The plaque gave a potted biography and his dates. While Jim and Pauline were fast asleep in their tents, I returned feeling surprisingly wide awake. We had a lengthy breakfast, during which we planned our next meeting in two days time at La Spezia, about 75 kilometres away. They were going to visit Pisa and Florence and I would walk to La Spezia, starting the following morning. The main road between Chiavari and La Spezia, the N. 1, was a meandering route which cut inland. I decided to try and cut the corners by following the coastline along what I then thought were path routes on the map.

When Jim and Pauline departed at midday, I tried to sleep, but it was too hot inside the tent and the insects kept me awake. I sat gazing over the bay and began to regret that I had done so little homework before setting off. The walk showed me my ignorance of so many things. I wanted to know how the mountains were formed, the history of the towns and villages I passed through, their legends and folk-lore. At night when the sky was clear I wanted to know more about the heavens. I prayed that, if I reach old age and am no longer physically fit for active work, my mind and memory may remain alive and that I may still have eyes that can see and ears that can hear. I could understand man's recurring belief in reincarnation because one lifetime can only be a beginning.

A thunderstorm began at 8 p. m. and lasted for two hours. Scottish thunderstorms are like Zeus gently clearing his throat compared to this full-blooded roar, and at one peal I thought I could feel the ground shake.

The sun was already warm when I left the terraced orchard to begin the 75 kilometres to La Spezia. At Sestri I stopped to change a traveller's cheque, a transaction which normally takes a few minutes. There was a queue at this bank which included an agitated American lady and I emerged an hour later. I was further delayed by a stupid mistake in map-reading, was chafing under the weight of the rucksack which I had not carried for five days and was growing irritable in the midday heat. A few kilometres beyond Sestri I left the main road and started on the short cut, the first 8 kilometres of which were through a disused railway tunnel. I took out my torch and entered, grateful for the sudden coolness.

For the first kilometre only a few cars passed but the tunnel began to turn and I could hear cars coming towards me and see the reflection of their headlights long before they could see me. The hot sun must have impaired my judgement at first, but now I realized the danger I was in. The tunnel had no light, no ventilation, barely provided enough room for two cars to pass and the edge on which I walked was crumbling and caused me to stumble. With a large rucksack it was impossible to get close in to the walls if a car came round the corner quickly. The traffic was increasing now, with a few manic drivers intent on reaching the end of the tunnel as quickly as possible. I wanted to turn back, but there was danger in this too, besides the loss of time and distance. After 2 kilometres there was a break in the tunnel and a parking place by the side of the road. On the rocks down below people were bathing. I sat on the rocks gulping the fresh air and then entered for the next 2 kilometres, meditating on darkness.

I thought of the darkness of death, death in my own family and the darkness into which it plunged the rest of us, a terrible darkness because I did not know whether I still believed in God or not. Part of me believed, part did not, and I did not know which part I was. I remembered, too, the darkness I had experienced when I went to Germany for my second year of theology studies. It was my sixth consecutive year of study, as I went straight to theology from Oxford, where my studies had included the modern English philosophers and their linguistic analysis, a course I had enjoyed, but which had left me incapable of understanding the scholastic theology which we had to study in Germany. I could recite the language of theology and manipulate it for examination purposes, but it left me unmoved and empty. There were periods of darkness later, especially in Glasgow when I heard that voice within me say, 'I don't think you know who you are.' I would never want those moments again, nor want anyone else to have them. Yet I am grateful for them because in the darkness I found a basis for faith which I could not find in the theology books. When I prayed in helplessness in the darkness I began to see a meaning in Christ's passion. He had entered into human suffering, our hopelessness, our darkness, our death and he shared in it. By thinking of this, I had glimmerings of light in the darkness and began to know that there are no depths where he is not and that for the Christian nothing can ever be hopeless. Emerging from the depths, I began to understand the resurrection not only as a past event for Christ and a future event for us, but as a present event for both of us. I remembered this as I walked the tunnel and grew less fearful of the traffic.

I emerged from the tunnel 8 kilometres after entering it and studied the map again for the remainder of the short cut. It was a small-scale map and the markings were not clear enough, so I made inquiries from a few passers-by who gave me long and, as far as I could understand it, conflicting advice, but the majority seemed to favour the main road. Their advice and a series of disastrous short cuts on the walk so far persuaded me to take the longer and safer route by the main road, which was 10 kilometres away and about 625 metres higher.

It was 7.30 p.m. before I reached the main road at La Baracca, where I had my first proper meal of the day. Two hours later I started looking for a place to camp, but the night was cool and clear so I kept walking till after midnight. The ground on which I pitched the tent was so hard that the pegs did not hold and the rear pole collapsed when I crawled inside. But I was too tired to pack everything again and look for another place and too uncomfortable to sleep where I was, so I snoozed fitfully for a few hours and then continued on the road for La Spezia.

At midday I came to a village on the hill overlooking the

beautiful bay of La Spezia where I had excellent *canelloni* and a carafe of red wine. I had walked 80 kilometres in the last twenty-seven hours, a personal best which I had no ambition to achieve and no desire to better.

As I was leaving the restaurant I asked the barman by the entrance if he could fill my flask with drinking water. As he was doing so, the manager appeared, took the flask from him, emptied it and handed it to me telling me I could find water in the toilets. Tiredness and frustration at my inability to tell him what I thought of him left me in a rage which the hot sun did nothing to alleviate. It was such a mean and unnecessary gesture and I could not forget it as I sat on a hillside outside the hotel trying to rest. I was feeling bitter, which was the real damage the proprietor had done me, so I looked at the bay and tried to drown my petty-mindedness in the immensity of the sea before me.

At 5 p. m. I started down the winding road into La Spezia to the station, where I was to meet Jim and Pauline at 7 p. m.

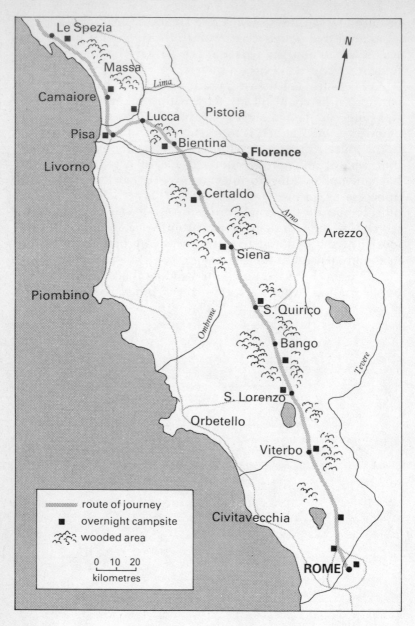

N

Le Spezia

Massa

Camaiore

Lima

Pistoia

Lucca

Pisa

Bientina

Florence

Livorno

Certaldo

Arno

Arezzo

Siena

Piombino

Ombrone

S. Quirico

Bango

Tevere

S. Lorenzo

Orbetello

Viterbo

Civitavecchia

ROME

route of journey
overnight campsite
wooded area

0 10 20
kilometres

La Spezia to Rome

10

Florence, Siena, La Storta

They were announcing train departures and arrivals at La Spezia station. Rome was only a few hours away and I had enough money to buy a ticket. The temptation was only the gentlest plucking at my sleeve and I dismissed it easily because my attention was on the road waiting for a white Renault, company at last, food and sleep.

'Do you know what happened to us at Pisa?' asked Jim, still in the car. 'Pauline, in her ankle-length skirt with sleeves down to the elbow, was not allowed to enter the cathedral because she was indecently dressed.' He also told me that they had found the ideal camping place in an olive grove high up in the hills, with a waterfall nearby and a derelict house with a wide verandah, which neighbours had told them they could use. He told me all this by way of apology that this paradise was over 64 kilometres away.

We drove though Pisa, saw the leaning tower and passed the cathedral on our way to the olive grove high in the hills. As we sat on the verandah having dinner, Jim launched into a tirade which began with Pauline's expulsion from the house of God and then developed into an indictment of the hypocrisy within the Catholic Church, her tendency to strain at gnats like Pauline's short sleeves and swallow camels like the evils of capitalism; her obsession with sex and blindness to social justice, her habit of laying heavy burdens on people's shoulders and then making them feel guilty at falling down under the weight. Indignation kept him going well after bedtime. With his red beard glinting in the light of the storm lantern, his hands waving and his blue eyes wide with anger, he sounded like Amos. But not even his eloquence or the importance of

147

his theme could hold back the waves of tiredness which were falling on me. I told them about the tunnels, my detours, the collapsed tent and my fatigue. They suggested that I come to Florence with them the following day and they would bring me back to La Spezia in the evening. I remember the rustle of the olive trees and then no more until nine the next morning.

Six hours is a ridiculously short time to spend in Florence, but long enough to understand why so many people have come, have seen and been conquered, living in the city for the rest of their lives.

Pauline, who had spent a summer in Florence a few years before, was an excellent guide. She did not lecture us, but gave a minimum of background information, pointed out occasional features of a building or painting and then left us to look in peace.

Although I had been too tired the night before to follow all the points of Jim's prophetic discourse, I had understood that bare arms and bare legs are banned in Italy's cathedrals and so I walked through Florence clutching a plastic bag containing a pair of slacks for emergencies. Jim, true to his principles, came bare-legged and entered the cathedral first. The doorkeeper rose like a startled partridge, flapped his arms and protested loudly in Italian. Jim continued his prophetic discourse of the evening before, in English. The doorkeeper belonged to that hard-necked generation which never did have any time for prophets. While Jim stood blocked by the powers and dominions of officialdom, Pauline and I, clothed according to regulations, slipped by feeling treacherous. After a brief visit, I offered Jim my trousers, telling him that he must not miss Michelangelo's later *Pietà*, but he made me feel like one of St Anthony's devils.

Of all that we saw in Florence in our brief visit, it was Michelangelo's *The Captives* which held me at the time and will always remain in my memory. As I stood staring at the figures of this unfinished work, Pauline told me that Michelangelo always worked in the belief that the forms lay hidden within the marble and that the art of sculpture was to allow these forms to emerge. Out of the great formless chunks the figures of the slaves were beginning to emerge:

head, shoulders, torso, straining to be free, but still held fast in the formless stone. A few yards further down the hall stood Michelangelo's *David*, carved as a symbol of Florence but also a symbol of what man can become when free of his enslavement.

I had often looked at sculptured figures and admired them, but for the first time in my life I could look at these figures and become them, share their hopes and frustrations and know the conflict within them. I could hear the voice of common sense saying to *The Captives:* 'What is the point in struggling like this? You'll never break free. Why impose this stress and strain on yourself, wear yourself out in useless striving? You need tranquillizers. Why not accept yourself as you are, deluded creature, sink back into the marble from which you came and stop tormenting yourself with impossible dreams? In the end you will have to do this, for you can never break free.' *The Captives* are tormented by this voice of reasonableness but they are driven on by an urge which is deeper than reason, to struggle to break free of all that holds them bound. They do not understand this urge, nor do they know what freedom will bring them; they only know that they cannot rest in this captivity and that to cease to struggle is to cease to be.

The Church exists to set us free, to encourage us to dream and then show us that our wildest dreams fall short of the reality which we can become. She exists to uncover the form that lies within us, to hold up before our eyes not the *David*, but 'the Son of David': 'Something that has existed from the beginning, that we have heard and we have seen with our own eyes; that we have watched and touched with our hands: the Word, who is life.' She exists to give us hope against the temptations of reasonableness and common sense. She is to be the 'Light of the Nations', showing them that the kingdom of God is within us and among us. She is there to interpret for us this deep instinctive urge to be free, to nurture and strengthen it, defend and promote it. In Jim's tirade of the evening before he was not really complaining about Pauline's exclusion from Pisa Cathedral because of her short sleeves, but he was asking, as so many other Catholics who are criticized for being critical are asking, for a Church which will give them hope in their struggle to be free.

We returned to La Spezia station at nine that evening and I said farewell to Jim and Pauline who were driving on to Rome. As their car disappeared from sight I heard the train announcements again. They were no longer a gentle plucking at my sleeve, but an insistent temptation, the voice of common sense and reasonableness. What was the point in continuing except to satisfy my own vanity and be able to say, 'I once walked to Rome'? The walk had been enjoyable so far, but the novelty had worn off and the weather was uncomfortably hot. Why not take the train to Siena, at least, and leave myself more time and energy to walk in the Tuscan hills?

In the *Spiritual Exercises* St Ignatius says that 'in desolation when the soul is wholly tepid and slothful, sad and separated, as it were, from its Creator and Lord,' one should not make a decision, nor go back on a decision already made. Although my present state did not merit such a grandiose description and I was merely tired and feeling lonely at being on my own again, I decided to walk myself into a better mood.

After two hours walking my mood had worsened. My map gave no details of the city and I meandered through its streets in the dark, trying to find a short cut to the main N. 1 for Rome. In Florence they have a saying, 'How much the fool who goes to Rome excels the fool who stays at home.' At the edge of the city I stopped at a cafe for a cup of coffee to keep me awake on the night walk. As I sat by a table on the pavement a heavy Italian approached. He stared hard at me, stopped, stared again at me, then at the rucksack by my chair, glanced at his watch for it was nearly midnight, touched his head with his hand and shook it in despair at my stupidity. I wished I had known the Italian for *d'accord* but I just stared back in sullen silence. When I did get clear of the city and on to the main road, the sky was dark and I kept stumbling, going over on my ankles on the uneven verge. I found a farm track to my left, followed it into a field and camped for the night, hoping that sleep would change my mood of loneliness and indecision.

Church bells woke me next morning at eight because it was

the feast of the Assumption of Mary. Half an hour later, being too late for Mass, I was on the road unwashed and unbreakfasted, in such a state that I was not sufficiently conscious to know how I felt. There was a fruit stall by the roadside selling melons and across the road a farm with a large trough in the courtyard. The farmer, when he saw me sitting in the sun by the side of the trough to breakfast after washing, invited me to use his summer house, a simple wooden structure covered in dried corn stalks. I asked him where I could find a church and the times of Mass. 'There are churches all over the place,' he said, 'but I don't go myself.'

There are various ways of overcoming desolation, the most common being 'wait till it passes', but I discovered a new way that morning and now recommend a melon; not a mere slice, but a whole melon. It worked wonders and by the last bite I was fully determined to walk every step of the way to Rome.

I kept trying churches for Mass, but the Mass was either just finished or I would have to wait a few hours for the next one. I tried to pray, but thoughts were getting in the way and I could not get started. The doctrine of the Assumption of Our Lady was nagging at me. In 1949 Pope Pius XII had declared Mary's Assumption into heaven after her death to be a defined doctrine of the Catholic Church. Since the declaration of papal infallibility at the First Vatican Council in 1870, this declaration of Mary's Assumption is the only instance of its exercise. The doctrine of papal infallibility is so heavily qualified in the text of Vatican I that it is very difficult to know what precisely it is saying, especially since the only instance of its exercise is in this doctrine, which is even more obscure.

While I was in Glasgow, I had been invited on one occasion to give a short retreat to the fifth form of a girls' school. One afternoon we had a question box. The girls wrote out questions and I tried to answer them. Things were going well until I unwrapped the last question. In beautiful italic script the questioner asked: 'In light of recent work on original sin, what are we now to make of the Assumption dogma?' It was an excellent question, which I could not answer, but it came back to me now on the road to Viareggio. Fast walking and theological questions do not mix well. I gave up thinking, prayed the Hail Mary in rhythm with my steps and began to calm down. Later in the afternoon I stopped for a swim in the sea and afterwards began thinking about the Assumption again.

I believe in God, but he is a transcendent God, the wholly Other, and therefore my belief in him allows me to be an agnostic and a believer at the same time. I believe he is 'the Way', not the end of the road, and so my faith does not give final answers to questions but the courage to face them. Belief in God is not primarily belief in a body of doctrine, but in God who communicates his life to us in every moment of our existence. He is 'Emmanuel', God with us, and there are no depths of our existence where he is not. I believe in the resurrection of the body and life everlasting. I cannot imagine what it will be like and I do not try to do so. I am much more interested in experiencing resurrection now in a life of freedom from selfishness, narrowness and the confine of my own fears. I believe that God calls us to be one with him, with ourselves, with every other human being, with all creation. I cannot believe that he created us for himself and has made us restless until we rest in him if at death we cease to be and are no more. The news is too good to end at death. I can understand the Assumption of Mary in so far as it is a reminder to us that we are all called to resurrection and that, of all creatures, she is the fairest and is at one with God in a way that is unique.

I walked barefoot from the beach to the main road and took great care to remove all the sand from my feet before putting on my socks, but after a few kilometres I could feel the rub of it.

The Italians seem to holiday in swarms, not just dad, mum and the kids, but uncles, cousins, aunts and grannies as well. I liked watching them go by as I sat outside a cafe, for Italians have an enormous capacity for enjoying themselves.

After nearly 48 kilometres in the heat I was searching for a place to eat when I passed a wood where hundreds of people were gathered, having a meal at trestle tables. There was an open-air kitchen at one end where I joined a queue. The menu of baked beans, sausage and fried bread was more like Glasgow University refectory than the Italian Riviera, except for the half bottle of Chianti which went with it. As I came up to be served, I noticed that all those in front of me were presenting not lire, but vouchers, and I was directed to a booth at the side. *'Non parlo bene Italiano,'* I began. 'That doesn't matter, comrade,' said the man at the booth in English, 'what would you like?' So I was given a voucher for 1,000 lire and exchanged it for a huge plateful of sausage, beans, fried bread and a half bottle of Chianti and sat down at one of the tables. As I ate, I wondered what kind of gathering this was. The people were in family groups, they all seemed to know each other and they were in a very festive mood. I thought it might be some kind of parish outing, a final celebration of Our Lady's Assumption, and was half expecting to see one of those soutaned, soup-plate-hatted Italian clergy. A small boy appeared at my side, asked me a question which I could not understand, then slapped a sticky badge on my shirt. It read *Festa dell' Unità*. I looked up and saw several banners hanging from the trees and bearing the same message. I had joined in the celebrations of the Italian Communist Party, one of a series organized throughout Italy.

I regretted my halting Italian, because I wanted to talk to the families around me and find out how they regarded the Communist Party. To judge from their faces at this meal, they thoroughly approved of it. As I walked through Italy, I saw the party's propaganda on many a billboard and support for the party by individual graffitists. The expressive genius of the Italian is still living and fills every blank piece of wall. All the *graffiti* I saw were political and gave the impression that political issues in Italy are remarkably simple. Either you are good and for justice, equality and the workers, or else you are a capitalist, imperialist pig. The inequality in Italy between rich and poor was very obvious. The Communists promise greater equality and to clean up corruption in government at local and national level. At local level they have shown themselves to be just and efficient administrators and they seemed confident of eventually winning a national election.

I was now on the outskirts of Viareggio and had walked 70 kilometres in the last twenty-four hours. Too tired to walk clear of the town before camping, I found a small plot of ground in a square of houses behind the promenade and slept there. Next day, August 16, I set off early for Lucca, hoping to arrive early enough to look at the city before camping, but the heat was as heavy as the traffic and the road was disfigured by huge, garish billboards advertising cars and drink. It was already dark when I left the restaurant in Lucca where I had stopped on arrival for a meal. Through France I very rarely ate in restaurants, but bought food and dined in the fields. In Italy I usually looked for a restaurant for an evening meal. Meat dishes were expensive, but *pasta* (especially if it was *cannelloni*), bread, cheese and wine made an excellent meal and cost little more than a supper from a grocer's shop.

As I left the restaurant I was trying to remember a Roman history essay which I had laboured over years ago on the significance of the Triumvirate's meeting at Lucca, but the activities of Pompey, Caesar and Crassus were lost in the depths of my memory. I was soon lost too in trying to find the route out of the city. I finished up on the city ramparts from which I could see the roads going south and east, and decided to camp for the night there under the trees.

At 2 a. m. I heard a car draw up near my tent. Someone approached, shone a torch into the tent and asked a question which I could not understand. The voice announced itself again and this time I did understand. The police had arrived and wanted to know how many of us were in the tent. Discounting the ants, my regular companions, I told them I was alone. 'Good night,' said the voice, 'and sleep well.' I did so until 7 a. m. and over a cup of coffee tried to decide what to do, revise my ancient history or march on to Rome. The deliberations did not take long. Some demon of haste had taken hold of me and I felt compelled to rush on.

As my map was insufficiently detailed to help me find my way to the main N. 439, I walked by compass, but after 8

154

kilometres I was not too sure exactly where I was. A small group of people were standing outside a church, so I changed into slacks, entered the empty church and took a seat at the back. It was still empty when the sacristy bell rang at ten and two tiny boys appeared leading a large, bull-like priest to the altar. On cue the congregation, which had been gathering outside, entered the church, all the men going to the front and the women to the back, crowding into the benches and leaving me, like a leper, in isolation in the back bench. 'The Lord be with you,' roared the celebrant. The congregation ignored the greeting, the men continuing their conversations, the women adoring one another's *bambini*. After the Gospel the priest bade us be seated, took his place at the pulpit and proceeded to bellow. The women were still intent on their children, admonishing them for not attending and for failing to keep still, while the menfolk, who had quietened down during the scripture readings, came to life again and resumed their conversations. One man, recognizing a friend across the aisle, went over to greet him. The priest continued his valiant efforts to save the souls before him but his message, whatever it was, was lost on them. The people of God seemed very much at home in their father's house!

After Mass I asked for directions to the main road and I either misunderstood or was misdirected twice. It was 2 p. m. when I found the main road, but it was too hot for walking and I rested for three hours in a vineyard before continuing to Bientina, where I had my first Italian *pizza*, fresh from the oven, which was opposite the restaurant entrance. It was already dark when I finished the meal and went in search of a place to camp. The sky was overcast and I shone my feeble torch to the side of the road looking for a level stretch of ground for the tent. I ended in a wood where the trees were so closely planted that there was room only for the inner tent.

The route I had planned to Siena was cross-country and avoided main roads. But in my meanderings from Lucca and in the afternoon heat I had only covered 24 kilometres the day before. The demon told me that main roads would be quicker and less tiring, so I left the camping place between the trees and walked 45 kilometres at a brisk pace, much

155

helped by frequent thunderstorms which kept me cool. I camped again in the darkness by the side of the road, but my sleep was broken by unearthly grunts and squeals. In the light of morning I saw that I was next door to a factory with a pig farm behind it.

Siena was only 40 kilometres away. The thunder had cleared the skies. I tried to keep my eyes on the hills at either side of the road, looking at the vineyards, cypress trees and the villages perched on the hilltops. The road itself was depressing with its traffic, billboards, waste paper and noisome smells from the ditches at the side. Beyond Certaldo I could see the towers and spires of San Gimignano high on the hills and regretted that I had not kept to my original route through that famous town. Beyond Poggibonsi I stopped at a farmyard for lunch and was soon surrounded by hens and cats, so hungry that they soon lost their fear of me and each other in their rush to eat. The farmer appeared leading in his oxen, unyoked them and sat with me. When I had exhausted my meagre supply of Italian phrases, he sat on in silence. Silence with a stranger is usually an embarrassment to be banished with words, but the farmer was a peaceful man and I enjoyed his silent company.

As I approached Siena, I knew that I had the physical energy to continue to Rome and could arrive in five or six days time, but I was hurrying too much, turning the walk into an endurance test, my mind felt benumbed and I could no longer pray. I decided to stay in Siena from the Tuesday evening until Saturday morning, August 23, see the city at leisure and write up the final instalment of my articles for *The Tablet*. On the outskirts of Siena I stopped at a cafe and drank two litres of lemonade followed by a litre of beer. I asked the barman if he could recommend a *pensione* or cheap hotel nearby. He looked at me as if to say 'You must be joking', asked me if I realized that this was *Palio* time and assured me that every available room in Siena was occupied. 'But there is a large campsite about 6 kilometres away,' he added.

I was dragging my feet when I reached the campsite, but it was well worth the effort. It was beautifully situated on a wooded hillside overlooking the city, had every facility and was not overcrowded. Each day I had a different set of next-door neighbours and spent the evening with them over a bottle of wine. There were two French boys who were hitch-hiking their way across Europe with so little money that they could only afford a diet of corn flakes and bread which they ate solemnly three times a day.

On another evening I met an Oxford undergraduate who was a Northern Ireland Protestant. I cannot now remember the details of our conversation, but I do remember feeling sad as he described his life there and I reflected on the damage that religion can do. Many commentators, particularly religious ones, maintain that the Northern Ireland conflict is not a religious issue and there is a sense in which this is true, but the fact remains that the two factions are referred to as Catholic and Protestant and religious denomination can be used to foment and exacerbate hatred. Certainly, there is need for a political settlement, but religious leaders, too, have a terrifying responsibility. It is not enough for them to make heart-rending noises deploring violence: they need to think and meditate on the roots of violence, for the roots can be in a religious education which makes the child think that he is right, has been given the truth and means of salvation and that those who do not share his views are not only wrong, but dangerous. To inculcate such ideas in an educational system which keeps Protestant and Catholic children physically separated is a contributory cause of the violence.

I wondered too that evening, what would happen if the most fanatically violent men on either side could be persuaded to sit in silence for an hour just looking at each other and opening their minds to each other and letting their minds go blank. Could they stand the truth of the experience as it dawned on them that the Protestant or Catholic is also a human being who is doomed to death, afraid, in desperate need of reassurance and affection; that the other is also a part of me and that his destruction is also mine? Our religion must start with a recognition of one another's humanity, otherwise it is not only a waste of time, it is positively dangerous. That is why Christ said that if on our way to sacrifice, we remember a quarrel with our brother, we must first go and be reconciled with him and then make our gift to God. The God whom Christians worship has identified himself with every single human being. 'As you do to one of these least,' said Christ, 'you do also to me.' The primary function of a Christian minister, whatever his denomination, should not therefore be to collect his people into their separate schools and churches, but to work to reconcile himself and them to their enemies so that all may worship together in Christ.

On another evening I met two English girls, both Oxford undergraduates, who talked for a time about Siena and then moved on to discuss their own degree work and their difficulty in finding a job which would satisfy them. They professed not to be interested in money or status and were looking for work in the Third World. Next day they departed for Florence and I sat outside my tent, thinking about our conversation of the previous evening. St Ignatius wrote that his Exercises are designed for those who want to 'rid themselves of all inordinate attachments and after their removal to seek and find the will of God in the disposition of their lives for the salvation of their souls'. Those two girls had said that they did not want to get caught up in the rat race, but rather to do something useful with their lives by enriching other peoples', which seemed to me to be a very good translation of Ignatius' forbidding sixteenth-century language.

A thought came to me which I dismissed at first as crazy. Why not take up walking as a serious occupation and spend the spring and summer months wandering from place to place like those early Celtic monks? I could stop here and there, chat to people in cafes and campsites and when I found someone who was genuinely interested, really searching, then I would keep contact with them and offer them a course in the Spiritual Exercises. The thought kept recurring later and I remembered Christ's words: 'And as you go, proclaim that the kingdom of heaven is close at hand.' The quotation conjured up images of solemn men wearing billboards announcing, 'The day of doom is fast approaching: prepare to meet thy maker,' and so I dismissed the thought again and began to see how conventional my thinking tends to be. I dismiss a thought as crazy because it is unusual or because other people are likely to think it crazy. 'The kingdom of heaven is close at hand.' It was close at hand in those two girls, who were really saying, 'What does it profit us if we gain the whole world and lose our souls?'

A few weeks after the walk was over, when I was studying in Rome, I came across a passage written by Father Jerome Nadal, one of the early Jesuits who had the best understanding of Ignatius and the *Spiritual Exercises*. Nadal was answering the question: 'To whom may the Exercises be given?' He maintained that they could be given not only to Catholics and Protestants, with whom differences in doctrine were to be avoided, but also to pagans, provided they believed in God as creator and genuinely wanted to discover his will. As I read more of these early Jesuits, of their wanderings from place to place, of their work in hospitals, their talking and preaching in the streets, I began to see that my idea of summer wandering was not so crazy after all, and it is still with me.

After breakfast on my first day at the Siena campsite I sat outside my tent with a notebook on my knees and tried to write. I covered several pages without completing a sentence or leaving a phrase unscored. I was still suffering from a kind of mental numbness and the more I tried to write, the less I could commit to paper. I abandoned the attempt, took a bus into Siena and spent the rest of the day there, wandering through its narrow streets, unchanged in centuries, until I came to the magificent *campo*, scene of the *Palio* a few days before.

During the previous days, whenever any Italians asked me where I was going and I answered, 'Siena,' they would look at me in surprise and say, 'But you'll miss the *Palio*.' The *Palio* is a famous horse-race which takes place around the feast of Mary's Assumption. The flagstones of the wide *campo* are covered in earth for the occasion which begins with a civic procession, the participants dressed in medieval costume. The city was originally divided into seventeen wards, each with its own church and its own coat of arms. The wards had names, reminiscent of boy cub groups: owls, geese, she-wolves, snails, dragons, caterpillars, etc. At the festival ten of the seventeen wards are chosen by lot to take part in the race. Before the race, the horse is taken into the church for a blessing! The winner of the race receives a banner, or *Pallium*, bearing the image of Mary. As I walked past the groups of people sitting outside the cafes on the *campo*, I could understand little of what they were saying, but I kept hearing the word *cavalli* (horses) as visitors and natives relived the race.

Next morning I made a second attempt on my writing, recording whatever thoughts came into my head and refusing to score out anything, however inane or irrelevant it seemed. By midday, sore and stiff from sitting on the ground with a notepad on my knees, I went to a nearby restaurant for lunch. There was veal on the menu and the price seemed reasonable. The waiter brought a huge portion of succulent veal. When the bill arrived, it was double the amount I had expected to pay. The waiter pointed out a squiggle, which I had failed to notice, against the meat prices, signifying that the charge was *l'etto*, i.e. per 100 grammes, and I had eaten three times that amount. However, the restaurant gave me value for my money by allowing me to sit on at a table on the verandah until dusk, where I completed two articles for *The Tablet*.

On Saturday, August 23, I left Siena early in the morning to begin the last 230 kilometres to Rome. The weather was cool for the first hour until the sun came up to promise another burning day but, as I sat by the roadside having breakfast after two hours walking, the sky became overcast and I could hear distant thunder. When the storm broke, I sheltered for forty minutes. There was no sign of a break in the leaden sky, so trusting that the storm could not last all day and that I could dry out before evening, I decided to walk. For the first few minutes I felt discomfort until I was thoroughly soaked, when I began to enjoy the wildness of the storm, shouting in competition with the thunder, counting the seconds between the lightning flashes and the roar, watching the patterns formed by huge raindrops as they bounced off the roadway in little showers of spray. 'Out of the tempest God spoke.' The phrase from Job kept coming into my mind, but he remained silent and I plodded on.

The rain continued for six hours until 4 p. m., when I stopped to eat for the first time since my breakfast of rolls and chocolate spread. I had no sooner set up the stove and laid out afternoon tea, which consisted of the remaining roll and chocolate spread, when the storm broke again. I packed hurriedly and kept walking until I reached San Quirico, 50 kilometres from Siena.

San Quirico is a walled town where I had been sure I would find a hotel for the night, but I could find nothing. The alternatives were either to buy food in the town and then go searching for a camping place beyond it, or else find a camping place in the town, where I could safely leave my tent and rucksack while I went for a meal in a restaurant. The second alternative seemed best and I walked through the town looking for possible camping places and asking various passers-by. They were all unhelpful, a few were suspicious-looking and one was aggressive, unlike most of the Italians I had met so far. It may have been the weather which was affecting their mood, or my dishevelled appearance, or both. Near the city walls I saw a children's playground, mostly under water by now, but there were a few islands of grass above the water-line and a few yards away there was a restaurant. After supper it would be dark so that I could probably camp safely in the playground and depart in the early morning before the town was awake.

The restaurant was empty when I entered and still empty when I left. The meal was like the inhabitants, uninviting and aggressive, the *pasta* as tasteless as the tinned turkey which followed, the aggression coming in a carafe of fierce red wine. A thunderstorm accompanied the meal and I sat watching the rain pour down and bounce off the pavement. At the end of the meal I suddenly felt ill and thought I would faint, breaking out in a cold sweat and feeling suddenly weak. All I wanted to do was to lie down until the sickness passed or until I died. I sat with my head in my hands in a curious state of detachment, wondering what my body was going to do next. After ten minutes and several glasses of water, the faintness passed. I paid the bill, went out into the storm, pitched the tent in the playground on one of the few patches of earth still visible above the waters and crawled in. Thanks to the heavy cagoul which I had brought with me I was able to keep all my clothing dry while putting up the tent. With a prayer that the turkey, red wine and San Quirico police would all leave me in peace, I lay down to sleep or die.

At six the next morning I awoke to the patter of rain on the tent and waited for it to stop which it did, three hours later. Of all the seventy days I spent on the road, that Sunday walk from San Quirico and the following day are the most hazy in memory. On the Sunday I walked 40 kilometres through desolate country, feeling slightly unwell. I had no appetite but an unusual thirst, and this was the only day of the whole trip when I could not find drinking water for many kilometres. Towards evening I stopped at a bar to have ice cream and beer, a disastrous mixture, which soon brought me to a halt for the night.

Next day I tried to pray as I walked and was disappointed because I could not. I tried not to think and to let thoughts come, but I seemed to have changed into a walking machine, occasionally counting my steps just to make sure I could still count. There was a moment of light at Acquapendente, when I stopped for lunch on the verandah of a hotel overlooking the town and gazed at the colours, the blue sky and the honey-coloured stonework of the buildings with their red roofs. Later that day I walked past the vineyards and saw the rich clusters of grapes hanging from vines which looked too old and too withered to produce any new life.

On Tuesday, August 26, I walked fast all day and was in Viterbo at 3 p. m. when a thunderstorm broke and raged for two hours. Abandoning my plan to continue to Vitrella, I found a hotel room for the night. Somewhere in Viterbo I lost my last two sections of map, but they were no longer important as I was now on the Via Cassia, direct to Rome.

I wanted to slow down and make my way through Tuscany in leisurely fashion because I was ten days ahead of my schedule, but I could not resist the urge to reach Rome as quickly as my legs would take me. Wednesday, August 27, was my last full day's walking and I covered 46 kilometres, leaving less than 30 kilometres to Rome. As darkness was falling that evening I passed a motel, booked in and paid for a bed before seeing the room, which was filthy with a blocked basin and damp bed. The fields would have been drier and cleaner, but I was too tired to set off again in the dark, spent the night in my sleeping bag and was away from the place while it was still dark at 5 a. m., for the last day of the pilgrimage.

As dawn broke in a pale blue sky I too came to life again after the darkness of the last two days, and I remembered that first morning on Eileach an Naoimh, when I sat shivering in the morning mist, feeling as grey as the sky until the sun broke through, lifting the mist from the island and from me. I knew that I must soon reach La Storta, a village outside Rome, famous in Jesuit history. I could see a hill on the horizon. La Storta must be there. When I reached the hill it revealed another plain with more hills on the horizon, and so I walked for three hours before I reached the village. Today I could pray again and I knew that in the dullness and tiredness of the last two days, he had been there all the time, the God who is always nearer to us than we are to ourselves, who is always greater than our moods. It is as though he plays with us, pretends to hide, then suddenly surprises us. When he returns, it is as though we have found him for the first time and everything changes.

Ignatius had travelled this road on his way to Rome in 1537. After completing his studies at Paris University, he left his first companions there, visited Spain and then went on to Venice where he waited for his nine companions to join him when their studies were finished. He had chosen Venice because they all planned to make a pilgrimage together to Jerusalem and perhaps stay there for the rest of their lives. In order to make such a pilgrimage, they had to have authorization from Rome, where they could obtain the necessary papers.

While waiting in Venice, Ignatius had met the Bishop of Chieti, Jean-Pierre Carafa, who was founder of a new congregation of priests called the Theatines. In 1536 Ignatius had written a letter to Carafa suggesting reasons why the new congregation was not increasing its numbers. One reason, on

Ignatius' analysis, was that the founder lived in episcopal splendour and not like a Religious in the spirit of 'St Francis, St Dominic and many other founders'. The letter was not well received. In that same year, Carafa became a cardinal and a powerful influence in Rome. Ignatius therefore sent his companions off to Rome to obtain permission for the pilgrimage while he remained in Venice, suspecting that his own presence in Rome would only jeopardize their chances. He was to suffer even more from that letter some years later, when Carafa had become Pope Paul IV.

His companions returned to Venice with papal permission for their pilgrimage, but the Turks and the Venetians were at war and there were no ships crossing the Adriatic. The first Jesuits then decided that if the war prevented their making the pilgrimage within a year, they would go to Rome and offer their services to the Pope, wherever he pleased to employ them. The war continued beyond the year and so in 1537 Ignatius with two of his companions, Laynez and Favre, set off for Rome and in October 1537 they passed through La Storta. While praying there, Ignatius had a vision in which he heard God say, 'I shall be favourable to you in Rome.' Later, he saw Christ with his Cross and the Father saying, 'I want you to take this man as your servant.' Christ then turned to Ignatius and said, 'I want you to serve me.'

Whatever the psychological explanation of this religious experience, it is very much in the spirit of his *Spiritual Exercises* written some years previously. The Exercises include a meditation, which he calls 'The Kingdom of Christ', which ends with a prayer, 'Eternal Lord of all things, this is the offering I make with your favour and help. I protest that it is my earnest desire and deliberate choice, provided it is for your greater service and praise, to imitate you in bearing all wrongs and abuses and all poverty, both actual and spiritual, should your most holy majesty deign to choose and admit me to such a state and way of life.' Later in the Exercises, he writes about 'three kinds of humility'. The third kind, which includes the first two, is a state in which, 'Whenever the praise and glory of the divine majesty would be equally served, in order to imitate and in reality be more like Christ our Lord, I desire

164

and choose poverty with Christ poor rather than riches; insults with Christ loaded with them rather than honours; I desire to be accounted worthless and a fool for Christ, rather than to be esteemed as wise and prudent in this world.'

He came limping into Rome in 1537, poor and powerless. When he died in 1539 his companions numbered over 1,000 and were known throughout Europe and beyond. I often wonder what he thinks of us today, and I wondered especially as I walked the road to La Storta. His first companions were gifted, highly qualified men, but they lived very poorly, did menial work in hospitals, taught poor children and gave all their services free. Today, why do we have to build large parish churches and live in presbyteries? In setting up new parishes, why don't we try to dispense with church and presbytery buildings, live in houses in which the poorest in the city live, take part-time jobs to earn subsistence money and spend the rest of our time trying to build up a Church which does not possess its own buildings, but is a Church of people, a community, which celebrates its unity in Christ in house Masses and, for larger occasions, hires a building? Why do we not abandon control and possession of our schools, colleges and universities, offering our services wherever the educational needs are greatest and living in community among the poorest in the city? Why charge for our services instead of relying on voluntary contributions? If contributions do not come, then we must either improve our services or abandon them and find some other form of service.

These vague thoughts occurred as I walked and I realized they were not practical. I also knew that part of me wanted them to remain that way, because I would be afraid of them in practice. But I prayed to dream more and for an understanding of poverty which was rooted in the love of Christ who is compassionate and therefore vulnerable. He suffered crucifixion because he became, in Paul's words, 'as men are', the poorest of men. In the catechism which I learned as a child the first question was, 'Who made you?', and the answer was, 'God made me'. This was followed by a bit of small print, which as eight-year-olds we had to learn by heart. It ran: 'GOD is the supreme Spirit, who alone exists of himself

165

and is infinite in all perfections.' I prayed to be delivered from any tendency to model my life on this God, the God of the philosophers and to find him instead in Christ who came to be 'as men are', to serve and not to be served.

In La Storta, where Ignatius had his vision, I sat exhausted and had breakfast on a litre of lemonade and a large ice cream, assuring myself that I would return to La Storta later to feed the soul. I was within 14 kilometres of Rome and could easily have arrived at St Peter's by early afternoon. The last village before Rome on the Via Cassia is Tomba di Nerone. At the end of the village stands the Scots College, a seminary for the training of Scottish candidates for the priesthood. I called in and introduced myself. The Rector, Monsignor Sean O'Kelly, welcomed me, invited me to stay for lunch, looked again and suggested that I might first like a bath. I had two baths in quick succession, the first in five weeks.

What a relief it was to know I had only one more hour's walking to do! I did not feel any tiredness now but rather the opposite. It was as though more life had been poured into me during the seventy days on the road. After lunch Monsignor O'Kelly, the perfect host, offered me a room for a siesta, which I accepted; but I could not sleep. I phoned the Collegio Bellarmino in Rome, where I had planned to stay, to let them know that I had arrived ten days early. The house was closed and would not open again until September. Monsignor O'Kelly invited me to stay at the Scots College until it opened, an offer I gladly accepted. I would do the final 6 kilometres into Rome next morning.

11

Down in the Engine-room: the Heart of the Matter

There is a saying, attributed to Monsignor Ronald Knox, 'If you are liable to seasickness on the barque of Peter, don't go down to the engine-room.' He was referring of course, to visiting Rome.

Leaving the Scots College on Friday morning to end my pilgrimage in St Peter's basilica, I hurried down to the Tiber, now a slow trickle of grey water flowing sluggishly under the Milvian bridge, and had my first view of St Peter's dome.

Pilgrim groups were already on the move, some Italian groups led by Don Camillo-like figures, wearing soutanes and soup-plate hats and holding banners aloft bearing the name of their town and patron saints in case their flock should stray in the streets of Rome. Other groups were led by more progressive priests, easily identifiable in their ill-fitting sports shirts and baggy trousers. I met one of these pilgrim leaders later, recovering his strength after leading a group of elderly English ladies on pilgrimage. Rome may require a lifetime to visit, but these ladies were determined to concentrate a lifetime into five days. They began the day with an early Mass to leave them plenty of time for sightseeing, which they continued through siesta time when the rest of Rome sleeps, returning to their hotel in the evening to compare notes on the beauty and atrocity of Rome. *Il padrone* of their hotel, a man who had seen the nations of the world in his dining room, marvelled at their energy and delighted in the amount of wine they would consume in place of pots of tea.

The traders were also out on the streets approaching St Peter's, their carts piled high with guidebooks, medals and mementos of Rome, Michelangelo's *Pietà*, St Peter's itself, the Colosseum, all available in pocket-size plastic. Business was brisk because this was the Holy Year, bringing a record number of visitors to the city.

The custom of declaring a Holy Year began, apparently spontaneously, on New Year's Eve, 1299, when a great crowd of people gathered in St Peter's hoping that a special indulgence would be granted at midnight. Pope Boniface VIII was at first surprised by this spontaneous gathering and consulted his advisers.

When a Christian confessed his sins and asked for absolution, the priest would impose a penance, which was understood to be a temporal punishment for the sins committed. Early penitential books by Celtic monks contain tariff lists for a variety of sins, listing the penalties appropriate to each. These penances were frequently so severe that Christians, rather than face them, preferred to delay confessing their sins until they felt that death was imminent, when absolution could be given without imposition of a penance, a practice which did nothing to improve Christian morals. It was this abuse which led to the introduction of indulgences, a practice with a sound doctrinal basis, the communion of saints.

Because we are one body in Christ, the health and goodness of one member can heal the weakness of others, but it was the application of this principle which led to abuses. The goodness of God, reflected in his saints, was thought of on the analogy of a bank account, so that the credit of the good could be transferred to the debits of the weak. Church authorities assumed the right to declare a valid transfer, provided the sinner was genuinely sorry for his sins and seriously intended a reform of life. The indulgence did not absolve the sinner; only God could do that, but it could remit the temporal punishment which the sinner had incurred. In so far as the practice can remind us that we need the help of others and can be helped by them, it could be of value: but it can also have the opposite effect and degenerate into an individualistic spiritual bargain-hunting.

A plenary indulgence was an indulgence which would cancel all the temporal punishment due to sins already

committed and was first given by Urban II at the time of the
crusades. 'Every man who sets out for Jerusalem with the
army to liberate the Church of God shall have the entire
penance for his sins remitted.' For two centuries only the
crusaders could gain indulgences, but on New Year's Eve in
1299 the crowds in St Peter's were asking for the same indulgence for themselves. Boniface VIII found a scriptural
precedent in the book of Leviticus. 'This fiftieth year is to be
a jubilee for you', when debts were to be cancelled, the land
redistributed, the Hebrew slaves set free. By February 1300,
Boniface VIII had declared that all who visited the Roman
basilicas during the year 1300 and made their confession,
would obtain a plenary indulgence. The word spread through
Europe. In Siena they inscribed the news on their cathedral
walls. 'Every hundredth year is held the Roman Jubilee. 'To
he who is penitent, all crimes are forgiven. Thus says
Boniface.' The pilgrims began to stream in: Dante is said to
have been among them. With the pilgrims came trade:
mammon was hard on the heels of piety.

The Holy Year was to be a centennial event, but Clement
VI held another in 1350 and later, Urban VI decided to
have them every thirty-three years in memory of the years of
Christ's life. They could be a means of Christian renewal:
they also brought wealth to an impoverished Rome. In the
fifteenth century, Paul II decreed that the Holy Year should
be celebrated every twenty-five years and Paul VI opened the
25th Holy Year in 1975 with a call for Christian renewal and
reconciliation.

I followed some pilgrim groups into St Peter's Square and
saw Bernini's colonnade which reaches out from St Peter's
basilica like two long arms welcoming all comers into the vast
square. Already, at 9.30 in the morning, the nations were
gathering, camera-bearing Asians, Africans in colourful robes,
Europeans, Americans. In the centre of the square stands an
Egyptian obelisk, which pre-dates the very founding of Rome,
and on either side of it are two large fountains.

Before entering the basilica I sat by one of the fountains
to collect my thoughts. In front was the entrance to St Peter's,
to the right the Vatican offices and papal appartments, above

169

was the pale blue canopy of Rome's morning sky. The sun was warm, not yet oppressive. All that I saw was pleasing to the eye and behind me I could hear the gentle spray of the fountain. I had walked 1,760 kilometres to reach this spot. At Vézelay, at Taizé, at other stages too along the road to Rome there had been unexpected moments when all that I had experienced, the pleasure and the pain, sorrow and gladness, loneliness and friendship, came together in a moment of great happiness and I had thanked God for his goodness. I was hoping for a similar experience at the end of the pilgrimage, but instead I kept thinking of a pagan poet's phrase and felt heavy within myself.

The Latin poet Lucretius devoted his life to liberating men from fear, which he considered to be the root of all evil. Man's fear, according to Lucretius, is not of death but of the torments which will be inflicted on him after death by the avenging gods for the sins committed during life. This fear drives man to behave inhumanly against his fellow man. Lucretius tells the story of Iphigenia's death. The Greek fleet, led by Agamemnon is on its way to Troy to rescue Helen. At the island of Aulis the fleet is becalmed. Agamemnon consults his seer, who tells him that he must sacrifice his daughter Iphigenia to the winds. Lucretius describes the death of this beautiful, innocent girl and ends with the thundering lines, *Tantum religio potuit suadere malorum* (Such evils can religion do).

This was the phrase which battered at my mind as I sat by the fountain and let loose painful memories of the cries I had heard from men and women, tormented by fear of what would happen to them after death and of the inhumanity which they practised against each other. Some were married outside the Church and were torn between love of their partner and fear of an everlasting punishment for this love. Others, married within the Church, felt they could not cope with any more children and practised contraception with guilty, fearful consciences, while others refused contraception although their partner wanted it, and their mutual love had grown into hate. I had met youngsters driven out of their Catholic homes by their parents because they would not attend Mass any more; they had grown embittered and had come to hate their Catholic heritage. There were so many others who had said, 'Religion has nothing to say to me: I'm much more interested in politics, in trying to work for justice in society,' and so they abandoned their Catholicism because to them it seemed to have nothing to contribute to their own and other people's real interests. They felt that the Church was too silent and timid in major matters of social justice, too compromised by the powers and dominions of this world to speak out against them, too busy with her own survival as an organization to have time for a wider world. I had heard such people described as rebels in the Church, victims of our permissive, materialist age and I seethed with anger.

'What the . . . hell do you want to go to Rome for?' the drunken student had asked me at the farewell party. More sober students asked, 'Why do you remain a priest within the Catholic Church?' I asked the question of myself.

I stay within the Catholic Church because the Church is a sign which points beyond herself, beyond her structures and formulations, her disciplines and laws, to Christ, the image of the unseen God, in whom all creation has its being and who is always greater than anything we can think or imagine. The Church points to him in Scripture, in her tradition, her liturgy and in the life of many of her members. She points to Christ, and in Christ I can catch glimpses of a hidden self, the self of which St Paul writes when he tells the Ephesians, 'Out of his infinite glory, may he give you the power through his Spirit for your hidden self to grow strong, so that Christ may live in your hearts through faith, and then, planted in love and built on love, you will with all the saints have strength to grasp the breadth and the length, the height and the depth; until, knowing the love of Christ which is beyond all knowledge, you are filled with the utter fullness of God.' I need these outward signs.

I am a sinner within a Church of sinners, and therefore it is not surprising that sinfulness should be manifest within the Church and should find expression within the very structures of its organization. We live in a sinful Church, a learning Church. That is why the Church is always in need of reform

171

and renewal, and it acknowledged this need in the Second Vatican Council. I acknowledge sinfulness within myself and within the Church. If I refuse to do so, I am being disloyal to myself and to the Church, because I no longer submit myself to the love and goodness of Christ and am in danger of changing the Church from being a sign of God's presence into an idol, a substitute for God. Idolatry was the temptation of Israel, of Christ in the desert. It is also the temptation of the Christian Church.

The Church points to Christ who calls all people to himself. It is therefore not loyalty but disloyalty to Christ and his Church to condone any tendencies within it to narrowness, sectarianism, bigotry. A loyal Catholic is neither suspicious of nor indifferent towards Christians of other denominations, people of other religions or of no religion: if we are loyal to the Church, a sign of Christ's love for all, we must go out to all, be ready to listen to them and learn from them. Christ came to bear witness to the truth. It is disloyalty to Christ and his Church to suppress or distort the truth in the interests of particular ecclesiastical plans or policies. Quietly to condone such behaviour is to perpetuate it. Christ came not to be served, but to serve. To oppose all forms of self-aggrandizement and triumphalism in ourselves and in the Church is to be loyal to Christ and his Church. Christ invites us; he does not coerce us. He encourages rather than threatens. He gave little detailed instruction about the future of his Church, but on one point he is unmistakably clear – on the exercise of authority among his followers. 'You know that among the pagans the rulers lord it over them, and their great men make their authority felt. This is not to happen among you. No; anyone who wants to be great among you must be your servant, and anyone who wants to be first among you must be your slave.'

The hierarchy and the clergy are servants of the people, the Pope himself is *servus servorum*, slave of the slaves. A servant must listen to the needs of those he serves. Bishops and priests are disloyal to the Church when they do not allow the laity to speak their minds, or fail to listen to them when they do speak. To accept and comply with clerical domination within the Church is to be disloyal to it and to Christ. He is the fulfilment of the prophets with their message of justice for men. Amos is typical when he preaches God's message to Israel: 'I hate and despise your feasts, I take no pleasure in your solemn festivals. Let me have no more of the din of your chanting, no more of your strumming on harps. But let justice flow like water, and integrity like an unfailing stream.' To be so immersed in inner church affairs that we have no time or interest for questions of social justice, to be so absorbed in self-reflection for self-perfection that we cannot see beyond ourselves is disloyalty to Christ and to his Church.

Christ saw the temple desecrated by money-lenders. He did not therefore abandon the temple, but cleansed it. Such behaviour cost him his life.

Because the Church is a sign of God's presence, whose ways are not our ways and whose thoughts are not our thoughts, it is therefore of the very nature of the Church that she should put our lives and our values in question. When she is true to herself and to the Gospel, her questions are uncomfortable, revealing and shattering our idols. If she is true to Christ, she acts as society's gadfly. Gadflies are brushed aside and killed, and Christ promised persecution for his followers.

I left the fountain and walked into St Peter's, entering by the door which is opened only for the Holy Year, a sign of God's continuous indulgence to us all. The basilica was already noisy with tourists. I sat near the altar built over St Peter's tomb. He came to Rome to tell them, in St John's words, of

> Something which has existed from the beginning, that we have heard and we have seen with our own eyes; that we have watched and touched with our hands: the Word, who is life. That life was made visible: we saw it and we are giving our testimony, telling you of the eternal life which was with the Father and has been made visible to us. What we have seen and heard we are telling you so that you too may be in union with us, as we are in union with the Father and with his Son Jesus Christ.

Peter came, poor and powerless, to announce the Good News

that the kingdom of God is not in bread and circuses, nor in exercising dominion over the nations, but that the kingdom is within reach of everyone and is to be found in the love that we bear one another. This message of love was subversive of law and order. It always has been, it always will be. Peter was put to death. The tradition continues.

I thought of my own family, living and dead, of my relations, friends, acquaintances who have given me so much and I thanked God for them.

'I don't think you know who you are,' Laura had said this to me eight years before, a comment which had disturbed and distressed me. Now at the end of the pilgrimage I could see the truth of it and thank God for it. It no longer distressed: it gave me hope and encouragement. I don't know who I am. None of us know who we are, because God created us for himself and we shall never know who we are until we are at one with him.

Lord save us from every form of certainty which can rob us of this precious ignorance. Help us to keep searching after you, our way, until we reach the end of the pilgrimage, when every tear will be wiped away and we shall know you, our God, as you are and in you be at one with ourselves, with all men, with all creation.